LURLEEN'S LEXICON

OF

LAVENDER LOVE

Lurleen Johnson
(assisted by Simona Connelly)
Front cover photograph by Sarah Halsted

Ah sure do wanna thank the following gals an' guys: Nicki Heels, Sarah Halsted, Julie Burr, Becky Smith, Frances Rush, Becky Rush, Debbie Cooper, Terry Bryan, Brian Williams, Gino Emmitt-Pearce, an' any other folk who Ah done shoved ma scribblin's infront'a!

Special thanks ta Sarah Halsted fer takin' all'a the right purdy snaps'a yours truly, an' JB's American Diner - trust me, their food is real good, an' nothin' like Hell's Kitchen!

This book is dedicated ta the LBGT (an' straight!) folk who make the world a better place!

Hey y'all,

The name's Lurleen, and Ah just wanted to explain how this here Lexicon came ta be.

Ah'm just an ordinary blue collar gal who was never much for book-learnin', and Ah'm kinda surprised at all this writin' I been doin', but the other night Ah was leavin' Hell's Kitchen (that's the truck stop where Ah tote burgers for a livin') with ma good buddy Glenn when some shit-fer-brains redneck called me a dyke an' Glenn a faggot! Well, after Ah smacked the sorry son-of-a-bitch upside the head with an empty Thunderbird bottle Ah got ta thinkin', who thought these words up in the first place? Where'd they come from? An' Glenn wanted ta find out exactly what did that guy with the red bandanna in his right back pocket want from him the other night?

So instead'a headin' back to ma trailer an' havin' a few relaxin' Pink Squirrels Ah saddled up ta that ole Innernet an' thought Ah'd find me out a few truths, an' here they are. Hope y'all learn a few thangs!

Lots'a lurve

5

☺ Folks with this here symbol are all ma personal heroes, so don't go gittin' antsy if your favourite ain't here!

☹ In ma opinion, these guys are just assholes, plain an' simple!

🎬 This is *Lurleen's* Lexicon, so all these movies are ma personal favourites. Other movies listed without this symbol ain't, but they're important.

A

ABSEILING LESBIANS

Back in the bad ole 1980s the Conservative government in the UK brought in a nasty lil law called **Section 28** (see '**S**' for more details) which got the gay community mighty riled, an' rightly so.

On 2 February 1988 a buncha brave lesbians helped protest this by sneakin' inta the public gallery in the House of Lords, shoutin' "it`s alright, we won`t hurt you!" an' abseilin' down, right inta the middle'a those dumb ole men! Way ta go gals!

ABSOLUTE CODE

When y'all respect folk an' don't let on ta all an' sundry that they're gay – unless they're self-hatin' closet cases who spread a load'a guff about gay folk who've got the guts ta come out, that is!

AC/DC

This here's a slang term for folk who like ta do it with both fellahs an' gals (though not usually at the same time).

ACT-UP

'Aids Coalition to Unleash Power', organization formed in New York City in March 1987 "as a diverse, nonpartisan group of individuals united in anger and committed to direct action to end the aids crisis."

ACTIVE

Someone who likes ta take the lead, an' Ah don't mean on the dance floor

ADMIRAL DUNCAN

On the 30 April 1999 in this gay bar in Old Compton Street, London, a nail bomb exploded, killin' three people (**Nik Moore** and **Andrea Dykes**, who died at the bar, an' **John Light** who died the next day).
The bomb was planted by an asshole called **David Copeland**, who'd already set off nail bombs in Brixton an' Brick Lane, which injured

over 60 people, as he hated black an' Asian folk as well as gays.
He got six life sentences an' Ah for one hope the Nazi bastard rots in jail.

AFFAIR
Back in the ole days gay guys used ta call their cutie-pies this.

AGENT PROVACATEUR
This here's another way of sayin' the guy checkin' out your goodies in the bathroom may be a pretty policeman – best all beware boys!

AIDS
Aids is short for Acquired Immune Deficiency Syndrome.

Aids is not a single disease or condition. Instead, it is a term that describes the point when a person's immune system can no longer cope because of the damage caused by HIV and they start to get one or more specific illnesses.

People do not actually die from Aids; they die from the cancers, pneumonia or other conditions that may take hold when their immune system has been weakened by HIV.

The term Aids is now very rarely used. It is more usual to talk of late-stage or advanced HIV infection.

(Ah couldn't have put this better maself, so Ah took it directly from the Terence Higgins Trust website: www.tht.org.uk)

ALTERNATIVE LIFESTYLE

Refers ta folk livin' an openly gay life.

ALTERNATIVE MISS WORLD

This lil beauty pagent dates back ta 1973, an' was started in Islington, London, by **Andrew Logan**, an' is for all non traditional beauty queens (includin' guys).

Bein' an 'alternative beauty' maself (shut ya mouth!) Ah for one am glad it exists.

AMAZONS

These gals were a race of female warriors from Greek mythology.

They were mighty fine hunters and fighters, an' it's said they even cut off one'a their titties ta improve their bow'n arrow skills. They only did the nasty with guys ta have kids, and even then only kept the girl babies.

AMBI-SEXUAL

Another name for guy an' gals who like *both* guys an' gals!

ANANDRYNES

This was a sect (not the creepy kind!) of lesbians started in 1770 by an' ole French gal called *Thérèse de Fleury*.

The gals had a big ole fight about whether gay guys could join, an' broke up the group in 1784, so nothing really changes!

ANDROGYNOUS

Someone who kinda looks like a fellah or a gal, or neither (comes from the Greek word meanin' 'man-woman'.)

ANDROTROPE

Back in 1946 *Kurt Hiller* thought it'd be kinda cool if gay gays called themselves this. The gay guys didn't agree, so no-one hardly ever used it again!

ARCTOPHILE

These guys have a thang for big ole hairy guys – *arcto* bein' the Latin name for bears

ATTITUDE

Some gay guys act like their shit don't stink, an' seem ta enjoy lordin' it over all other folk. Come on now guys, there ain't no-one out there who's perfect, no matter what y'all may think!

AVERSION THERAPY

Ornery ole practise that's used ta try ta make gay folk straight, either by showin' 'em pictures and movies an' electroctin' 'em at the same time ta make 'em scared' an' sick 'cause'a the feelin's they git, or ta drug 'em ta git the same result.

Now Ah kinda thought that this was somethin' that only happened in the dark ages, an' while it's now rightly illegal in many places, folk in Arizona, USA, were still doin' it as late as 1992!

B

BDSM

This here stands for bondage, domination, sadism an' masochism, an' can cover all kinds'a sexual goin's on – from folk bein' tied up, whipped an' playin' in leather - ta other thangs that sound kinda scary ta ma mind (see '*Operation Spanner*') but are probably a hoot if that's the kinda thang y'all like. (There's a whole buncha further info in the 'S' section too!)

BABY-DYKE

Lil lesbian who's still a young'un.

BACKROOM

This is a lil dark ole room in the back of a gay bar where all kinds'a innerestin' thangs can happen!

BACKROOM BOYS

Gay guys who seem ta spend all'a their time in the backroom.

BARE-BACKING

Some folk are just plain dumb, an' even now still have anal sex without usin' condoms. Boys, git wise an' *rubber up!*

BANTON, BUJU ☹

In 1992 this guy released a song called **'Boom Bye Bye'** with the followin' lyrics:

Anytime Buju Banton come

Batty boy get up and run

Ah gunshot in ah head man

Boom bye bye boom

Goodbye, goodbye

Inna batty boy head

Rude boy no promote to nasty man

Dem hafta die

Which, thank the stars, led ta outrage around the globe, with his shows bein' boycotted an' all, but it kinda gits me thinkin', why do folk kick up a fuss when this guy (an' others) sings this kinda stuff, but when its inna 2000 year old book (see *Bible, The*, below) we either don't do diddlysquat, or we form our own Christian church (see *Metropolitan Community Church* – sorry guys, Ah just don't git y'all)

As a bit'a good news ole Buju done signed a declaration in July 2007 statin' that he won't be singin' his nasty ole gay-hatin' words no more, thanks ta pressure from the gay rights group *Stop Murder Music.*

BASIC INSTINCT

Back in 1992 we found summat else ta bitch an' moan about when this movie by *Paul Verhoeven* (director) an' *Joe Eszterhas* (writer) came out. Ah'm just kiddin'! We rightfully protested 'cos the movie showed two thangs, *Sharon Stone's* cooter, an' that bisexual women are murderin' psychos, which just ain't cool, or true! An' the movie was a crock of shit anyhow

BASTER-BABIES

Kids born (mainly) ta gay gals who've got kind'a inventive with the kitchen utensils!

BATH-HOUSE

These'a saunas where gay guys meet an' greet, an' have a good ole time (play safe boys!)

BATTY BOY

Caribbean slang word for a gay guy (not nice) – come's from the Jamaican word for butt.

BBC NEWS

Those cool abseilin' lesbians were at it again on 23 May 1988, when they invaded the six o'clock BBC News.

Annie King handcuffed herself ta news reader **Sue Lawley**'s desk an' the protesters shouted "stop the clause" (Section 28 was still a clause back then), givin' very public attention to this thick-headed legislation

BEAR

Big ole hairy guys, sometimes in leather britches.

BEARDS

If y'all don't wanna let on that you're gay this is a date of the opposite sex who shows up with y'all at public events so's y'all can stay in that ole closet.

BECHDEL, ALISON ☺

Ah lurve comic books, and this gals *'Dykes to Watch Out For'* series is one'a the best Ah've ever read.

Ya git whiney ole Mo, practical Harriet, sexy Lois, an' family types Clarice an' Toni, all livin', lovin' an' sometimes fightin' in their close-knit community.

Alison sneaks in loads'a political stuff that'll broaden ya mind while ya chuckle at the gals antics.

She's also writ herself two books, *Fun Home*, an' *Are you my Mother*, which'll give y'all an insight inta her life.

BIBLE, THE

Whoever writ the Old Testament sure hated gay folk!

First of all you've got that ole tale of Sodom in *Genesis* (19: 4-8), then ya got *Leviticus* (18:22) sayin': *'thou shalt not lie with mankind, as with womankind: it is abomination.'* and (20:13) *'if a man also lie with mankind, as he lieth with a woman, both of them have committed an abomination: they shall surely be put to death; their blood shall be upon them.'*, which kinda puts it bluntly!

Mind, these are the same folk who say y'all can't have a bowl'a clam chowder for dinner, but its fine ta eat beetles an' grasshoppers!

BICURIOUS

Ah personally hate this here term, 'cause y'all usually see it in personal ads, an' it kinda seems ta mean a straight gal who'se boyfriend would like ta see her git down an' dirty with another gal – but Ah guess Ah'm just bein' narrow-minded.

BINDING

This is when a gay gal straps her titties down with tape or a bandage so as ta look more like a guy.

BISEXUAL

See *AC/DC* and *Switch-Hitter.*

BLACK TRIANGLE

Symbol used in Nazi concentration camps ta identify lesbians an' other 'anti-socials'.

BLUE

Russian folk call gay guys "goluboy", which is also their word for the colour light blue, an' the colour was also used by Italian writer **Dante Alighieri** ta symbolise the sin'a lust in his book '**The Inferno**'.

BOI

This git's kinda confusin', as it means both a cute young guy an' a dyke bottom, so y'all might want'a double check when y'all reply to a personal ad folks!

BOSTON MARRIAGE

This is when two gals live together an' all, but don't git down an' dirty, or ever have.

Some folk say the term comes from '**The Bostonians'** by **Henry James**, which was writ in 1886 about feminism an' what-not. In the book Olive Chancellor an' Verena Tarrant live together until Verena runs off with Olive's cousin Basil Ransom (dumb gal!) an' none of 'em live happily ever after.

BOTTOM

Someone who don't like ta take the lead durin' sex. Known as a **catcher** in the U.S.A, - an' just plain lazy in ma trailer! (Just kidding folks!)

BREEDERS

Slang term for them crazy straight folk – thought it seems ta me that gay folk are doin, more than their bit in that department too nowadays!

BRIGHTON

Gayest city in the United Kingdom (after London), an' where Ah call home.

BROILER

Kind'a mean, but this is chicken that's gotten a lil older an' can't quite pass no more.

BRONSKI BEAT ☺

This cool electro three-piece from Scotland were the first ever openly gay pop band, an' wrote some great songs like *'Smalltown Boy'*, an' *'Why?'*.

BROWN, RITA MAE

Rita wrote a great, gritty lesbian novel, **'Rubyfruit Jungle',** but will forever be remembered in this trailer park as the woman who, in 1981, tried ta blow Martina Navratilova away with a hand-gun when she dumped her!

BROWN FAMILY, THE

Gay folk in the 1940's were said ta belong ta this family, mainly 'cause everyone seemed ta think (an' some still do!) that all gay guys are innerested in is each other's butts, which ain't always the case as we all know!

BRYANT, ANITA ☹

Another jerk for Jesus!

In 1977 when Florida wanted ta start treatin' gay folk right, Ms Bryant decided we were sinful, an' after the kids (**'the recruitment of our children is absolutely necessary for the survival and growth of homosexuality'** – that's her quote, not mine!), so she formed **Save Our Children** in Miami to peddle her tired ole shit.

We got mad, stopped buyin' orange juice from the State, an' (provin' there *is* a god with a sense of humour!) someone threw a banana cream pie in her face in Des Moines, Iowa.) In the end she lost her job with the Citrus Commission, her husband dumped her, an' gay folk finally got rights in Florida (though not til 1999).

BUG-CHASER

Ah cannot git ma lil ole brain 'round these folk! They're HIV negative fellahs who look for guys who're HIV positive, or with aids, in order ta contract the disease. Why, why, why?

BUGGER

Sorry ta be crude, but this means takin' it up the ass.

The word itself may come from a French Christian sect called the **Bogomils** from the 1030's, who are said ta have done this so's not ta git their womenfolk pregnant (that was their story anyhow!)

BUGGERY

See above

BULL-DYKE

Big, tough ole lesbian.

24

BUNGIE BOY

This is a gay or bi guy who acts kinda straight, an' thought some folk think it means goin' from one place ta another (like bungee jumpin') its origins really come from navy slang for a gym teacher, an' also an ole word for a rubber, or condom.

BUNKER

When guys (gay *or* straight!) git sent ta prison all kinds'a thangs go on, an' this is what it's called when they'all git close an' personal with a cell-mate.

BUNKER SHY

This is a guy who's ascairt'a gittin' close an' personal with his cell-mate!

BUT I'M A CHEERLEADER 🎬

One a ma favourite movies!

Megan's mom'n dad think she's a lesbian, so they send her off ta "straight camp" ta git her fixed. Course, once she's there she realises she really *is* a gay gal, an' falls in lurve.

Real sweet, funny, an' *very* pink. Starrin' **Natasha Lyonne**, **Clea Duvall**, **Rupaul** an' the fabulous **Mink Stole**

BUTCH

Big, tough ole lesbian, who usually likes ta lead (an' this sometimes *does* include dancin'!).

BUTT-PLUG

Lil bitty (tho not always!) Bit'a rubber that y'all shove up ya ass!

BYKE

Some gals can't make up their minds if they prefer other gals or guys, an' this is one who says she like's gals, but still keeps the boys around too!

C

CAMP

A gay guy who acts a lil bit theatrical, wearin' colourful clothes, bangles an' bows – well, not really but y'all git what Ah mean.

Can also mean tastefully tasteless, like the pink flamingos on the lawn in front'a ma trailer.

The word comes from the ole French sayin' **se camper,** which literally means ta act all exaggerated an' over the top.

CAMPER, JENNIFER ☺

This gal is another cool comic book writer, with sexy, sassy gals' gittin' up to the dickens in most'a her work. Check out titles like '**Rude Girls and Dangerous Women'** or '**Subgurlz'** ta git ya box buzzin'!

CAMPFIRE GIRLS

Slang term for gay gals, taken from the totally ungay youth organisation founded in 1910,

thought their motto is *"give service"*.
Hmmm....

CATAMITE

This is an ole term for a young gay guy who's gittin' some good lovin' from an older guy.

The name comes from a translation'a the name **Ganymede**, who was a Greek guy from ancient times who sure knew a lot about that kinda thang – he's said ta have gotten it on with many a guy, includin' king'a the Greek gods, **Zeus** himself!

CAMPAIGN FOR HOMOSEXUAL EQUALITY

Allan Horsfall an' **Tony Dyson** formed the **North-Western Homosexual Law Reform Committee** on 4 June 1964 in Manchester, UK.

The guys main aim was ta git the British government ta change their foolish ways an' let gay guys love each other without havin' ta fear gittin' jailed for it, an' when this finally happened in 1967 they changed the name ta the **Campaign For Homosexual Equality,** who have carried on fightin' for rights an' freedom for gay guys and gals ever since.

CHICKEN

Young gay guy

CHICKEN QUEEN

Gay guy attracted to chickens (see above).
Known as a 'chicken hawk' in the USA.

CHRISTOPHER STREET WEST

This here's the address of the Stonewall Bar
(see '**S**') an' on June 28 1970 it was the name
gay folk in the USA used for the first pride
parades in cities across the country ta
commemorate the historic happenin's in New
York City the year before.

CHUBBY CHASER

Gay guy or gal who likes 'em big an' cuddly.

CIRCLE JERK

This is kinda like a sexy game'a pass the
parcel, when a bunch'a gay guys all sit around
in a circle an' have a mighty good time!

CIRCUIT PARTIES

These shindigs are big ole events that first
started in the 1970s, where gay guys go ta
boogie, cruise an' have a good ole time.

CIVIL PARTNERSHIP

The Labour government in the UK finally got with the programme an' let gay folk tie the knot (well, almost) in December 2005. Things got even better in 2014 when marriage became legal for us gay folk in the UK (see "*Gay Marriage*")

CLEAR

This is a guy who's only ever been innerested in guys, or a gal who ain't never played hide-the-wiener with a guy!

CLONE

This here's a gay guy who likes ta wear checked shirts, blue jeans, an' a lil ole moustache – the term referrin' ta the fact that they all looked pretty much alike!

They were all the rage in the 1980s but y'all don't see so many nowadays.

CLOSET

If y'all don't wanna let folk know you're gay y'all hide in the closet.

COCK RING

A lil ole piece'a leather or metal that guys put on their dicks ta keep all the blood in for lots an' lots'a fun.

COMMITMENT CEREMONY

When two gay guys or two gay gals want'a show their kith an' kin just how much they love each other this is what they do, especially those folk who live in dumb ole countries who won't let 'em legally tie the knot (an' y'all know where Ah mean!)

COMING OUT

If y'all *do* wanna let folk know you're gay y'all come outta the closet (it gits kinda cramped in there).

CONDOM

This here latex sheath keeps all the gloop in durin' sex, prevents all kinds'a nasty infections, an' is even used ta stop straight gals from gittin' pregnant!

CONSENTING ADULTS

Back in 1967 the Brits decided that gay guys could finally be together an' not git thrown in jail for it (see '*Wolfenden Report*') – but only providin' they were over 21, an' both agreed ta it – Ah don't have a problem with the last part, but the age thang was kinda dumb!

COOPER, FIONA ☺

Ah lurve this gal's books, especially *'Rotary Spokes'* (which Ah'm the proud owner'a a signed copy'a!)

Fiona appreciates the trashy side'a life in the U.S. of A, and knows a good drag queen when she sees one!

CO-PARENTING

This is when two gay guys, or two gay gals, git together an' have young'uns.

COTTAGE

This is what gay guys in the UK call a public bathroom where they'all can find more than the usual relief! Its cause they used ta look kinda pretty, with thatched roofs an' whatnot. (Known as *Tea-Room* in the United States)

CROSS-DRESSER

See *Transvestite*

CRUISE

Ta go out an' about lookin' for lurve, or somethIn' like it!

CRYSTAL METH

This nasty ole junk is becomin' the most popular drug with gay guys, an' lemme tell ya, that is *not* a good thang!

Its real name is *methamphetamine*, an' after a while it can make ya lose ya teeth, become impotent, psychotic, ruin ya immune system, an' will eventually kill ya.

CUNNILINGUS

Eatin' pussy. Comes from the Latin words *cunnus* (vulva) an' *lingere* (lick)

CURVE

This is a mag for gay gals, which was started in San Francisco, in May 1991.

It was originally called **Deneuve,** but French actress **Catherine Deneuve** got all uppity in 1995 when she realised she shared her surname with them (she sure is a slow reader!)

Her excuse was she was bringin' out a perfume with the same name an' thought folk would git confused an' not know a bottle of scent from a glossy magazine (guess she figures her fans are as dumb as she is!)

D

D & S

Yet another off-shoot of S & M (see '*S*'), this here means domination an' submission, so folk inta this are real quiet an' like ta do what they're told!

DADDY

This is what an older gay guy or gal can be known as by their younger sweetie-pie.

DAPHNIS

This guy was a shepherd in Greek mythology who loved guys an' gals, but had a special place in his heart for a fellah by the name'a Ganymede.

Many folk have told the story'a Daphnis an' his loves, includin' the poet **Richard Barnfield,** who writ the '***The Affectionate Shepheard'*** in 1594.

DANA INTERNATIONAL ☺

This gorgeous gal won the Eurovision song contest for Israel in 1998 with the song **'Diva'**, an' the twist was she used ta be a guy! But dang, if more gals looked (an' sang) like her Ah'd watch that damn contest every year!

DAUGHTERS OF BILITIS

It may sound like summat y'all can catch from a badly cooked burger, but this here is'a lesbian organization that formed in 1955 in San Francisco, an' took its name from **Pierre Louy's** book **'Song Of Bilitis'**, which contained lurve poems between gals.

DAVIES, RUSSELL T ☺

Born on 27 April 1963, in Swansea, Wales, Russell is an openly gay guy who wrote the TV show **'Queer As Folk'** in 1999, an' then brought **'Dr Who'** back ta the BBC in 2005, thrillin' folk (queer or otherwise) up an' down the UK.

DEGENERES, ELLEN ☺

What can Ah say about Ellen?

She broke ground by comin' out on her popular TV show, *'Ellen'*, which aired from 1994 ta 1998. Showin' an ordinary gal discoverin' her gay side was too much for some stupid folk though, so it got axed by ABC (they got a problem with gay folk? See *'Roseanne'*).

She then went on ta become a successful talk show host with *'The Ellen DeGeneres Show'*, which ta date (2014) has won eleven Daytime Emmy awards, so Ah guess she showed them dumb-asses in the end! Go git 'em gal!

DENTAL DAM

Lil ole piece'a latex used as safe-sex aid during cunnilingus.

DELARIA, LEA ☺

Oooh Lea! This gal is a big ole dyke, comedian an' jazz singer. She's wicked funny (check out her book *'Lea's Book of Rules for the World'*, if ya ain't an uptight ass) an' can now be seen struttin' her stuff in the fabulous TV show

Orange is the New Black. There'll always be a Pink Squirrel on offer in ma trailer if she cares ta come by!

DESERT HEARTS 🎬

This lesbian movie (based on the book *'Desert Of The Heart'* by **Jane Rule**) came out in 1985 an' it might be kinda dated now, but it sure is fun tryin' ta figure out how Cay (played by the gorgeous **Patricia Charbonneau**) gits undressed, inta bed, an' puts her clothes in a neat lil pile in about 5 seconds flat! It's also a very good movie!

DESPERATION NUMBER

This is a kinda nasty term for that guy or gal who looked as ugly as homemade sin when y'all first stepped inta the bar, but gets ta look might fine just afore closin' time!

DIESEL DYKE

Big ole butch lesbian, some'a whom drive trucks, hence the 'diesel' reference.

DILDO/STRAP ON

Fake dick, usually made'a silicone, which looks an' smells way prettier than the real thang, an' stays hard no matter how many Pink Squirrels ya have. Y'all can strap it ta yaself with a harness.

Some folk reckon the dildo gets its name from an ole song called '*the maids complaint for want of a dil doul'*, where a gal feels down-right sad, an wants ta be filled up with one, though in this case dil doul literally means an erect dick, so Ah guess she wasn't no gay gal. Ah kind'a like another idear, that it comes from the Italian word '*diletto'*, which means summat ta delight y'all.

DILLY BOY

This here's a Polari term (see '*P'*) from the 1930's, an' it means a guy who goes with other guys for money, 'cause back in the 30's a whole bunch'a 'em hung out in the Piccadilly Circus area in London, UK.

DIMASSA, DIANE ☺

Did Ah mention that Ah lurve comic books? Diane created 'homicidal lesbian terrorist' *Hothead Paisan,* who goes around beatin' up on assholes (usually guys) an' dances with her cat, *Chicken*.

DINAH SHORE

The lady herself was a big band singin' star in the 1940's an' 50's, but her name (for gay gals anyhow!) now mean's the big ole golf tournament in Rancho Mirage, California, USA, which goes on every March, an' which she started in 1972.

Nowadays gay gals head on down there ta party an' carry on, an' most of 'em don't seem ta give a hoot about woods an' nine-irons!

DINK

This here stands for 'Double Income, No Kids', which some gay folk seem ta be, though it ain't always so of course!

DISH

Folk who like ta spread everyone else's business around, come's from the expression "ta dish the dirt"

Can also mean a cute guy or gal, in that folk would like ta eat 'em all up!

DITTO, BETH ☺

Born in Arkansas, USA in 1981 (in a trailer, no less!) Beth may still be a young'un, but she's shapin' up ta bein' one'a the coolest gals on the planet! Aside from makin' some mighty fine music with punk/disco band *Gossip*, Beth's an out an' proud gay gal, an' fights the good fight for queer folk, fat folk, feminists an' non-conformists everywhere.

In 2006 she was voted top place in the British music mag **NME's** cool list (the first time ever for a gal), an' nominated by the same mag for sexiest gal in rock music.

Her outspoken, uncompromisin' way's – as well as her fantastic singin' voice – have gotten her praise from folk the world over, an y'all can expect ta hear way more from her in year's ta come, 'cause this gal's a goddess in the makin'!

An' Ah gotta add that she's as cute as a button, an' is always welcome in ma trailer, tho Ah kinda missed the boat as Beth done wed her honey **Kristin Ogata** in 2013

DIVA

This is a British mag for gay gals, which started in 1994, an' is still goin' strong

DIVINE ☺

Glenn Harris Milstead was born in Baltimore, Maryland, on 19 October 1945.

He became Divine in the 1960s, meetin' up with fledgling movie director **John Waters,** an' starrin' in many of his movies, such as **'Pink**

Flamingos', 'Female Trouble', an'
'Hairspray'.

He also had a bunch'a club hits in the 1980s
with songs like *'Shoot Your Shot'*, *'You Think
You're A Man'* an' *'I'm so Beautiful'*

He was about ta start work on the hit TV show
'Married with Children', in a longed for male
role when he sadly passed away on 7 March
1988. R.I.P. Divine

DON'T ASK, DON'T TELL

Back in 1993 Bill Clinton took a break from
smokin' cigars ta bring in this lil rule for the US
military.

Basically it meant that gay folk could be in the
armed forces, but they weren't s'posed ta let on
that they *were* gay.

DRAG

Folk reckon that drag used ta be writ on
William Shakespeare's scripts as a stage
direction, meanin' that one'a the actin' folk takin'
the stage was a guy who **dr**essed **as** a **g**al.

DRAG-KING

This is a gal who dresses as a guy, mainly
'cause she thinks it's a hoot.

DRAG-QUEEN

This is a guy who dresses like a gal, an' usually performs a cabaret act.

Famous drag-queens include **Dave Lynn**, **Lily Savage**, an' **Maisie Trollette.**

Ah ain't no drag queen, Ah just dress like one!

DUTCH BOY

This is a straight guy who likes ta hang out with gay gals (as friends, of course!)

It comes from the tale of '**The Little Dutch Boy'**, which was writ by **Mary Mapes Dodge** in 1865, though if any guy tried ta stick his finger in this here dyke he'd git himself a busted head!

DUTCH GIRL

Like the thang above, this means a gay gal

DYKE

Term for a gay gal, which folk think has its roots in Greek mythology, comin' either from **Dike**, who was the virgin Greek goddess of justice, or from **Dictynna** or **Dicte**, who didn't like guys, an' threw herself from a cliff rather than git bothered by Minos, the king of Crete. (Ah

43

always find a kick in the balls works better maself!)

DYKES ON BIKES

Big ole gals on Harleys! Yeh baby!

The Dykes on Bikes gals formed in 1976 at **Amelia's** bar in San Francisco ta ride in the city's Gay Pride.

Any room on ya pillion for a big haired gal in sling-backs, honey?

DYKE POTENTIAL AKA D.P

If y'all see a cute gal some'a y'all will wonder ta yourself "is she or isn't she?", (an' Ah ain't talkin' about wearin' hairspray!) an' how likely it is that she's one'a the family.

E

EASTBOURNE TENNIS TOURNAMENT

This here tennis tournament from Aegon International is held in Eastbourne, UK, every June, an' used ta be a big ole dyke-fest, on an' off the court, so it's kinda a shame that the folks runnin' it decided ta let guys play too, which Ah reckon kinda ruins the vibe.

EFFEMINATE

A guy who acts kinda girly, comin' from the word 'feminine'.

ELIZABETHAN

Back in the 1960s some gay gals didn't like the word 'lesbian' ta describe themselves, so they'all decided they'd be known as "Elizabethans" - mayhap 'cause they'll liked the style'a clothin' from the 14th an' 15th century, though Ah can't rightly figure out why!

EMINEM ☹

This guy gives trailer trash a bad name.

Ever since his break-through single **'My Name Is...'** (which contains reference to him 'rapin' lesbians') he's been spreading hatred an' homophobia - not to mention misogyny – to kids the world over. His attempt to clean up his act by performin' with Elton John don't do much ta make up for these lyrics (taken from the song **'Criminal')**:

My words are like a dagger with a jagged

edge

that'll stab you in the head

whether you're a fag or lez

or the homosex, hermaph or a trans-a-vest

pants or dress - hate fags? The answer's

"yes"

homophobic? Nah, you're just heterophobic

ENTRAPMENT

This is when a good lookin' guy gives a gay guy a flash of the goodies in a cottage, an' then arrests him for bein' innerested!

EONISM

Chevalier D'eon was a French guy born in 1728 who had a mighty innerestin' life! He was a spy, a diplomat, an' in 1777 (either as part of a spyin' mission, or just 'cause he felt like it!) He started dressing as a gal called **Chevaliere Charlotte D'eon**.

She was so convincin' that folk got mighty confused, an' it wasn't until he died in 1810 that everyone realised she was a he. His name lived on for many years ta mean a guy who dressed as a gal.

EPICENE

This is someone that's a lil bit guy, an' a lil bit gal, an' comes from the Greek word **epikoinos,** which literally means somethang that's kinda like somethang else.

EQUAL AGE OF CONSENT

Most folk legally git to do it when they're sixteen, but for years gay guys in the UK weren't allowed to until they were 21. They were finally made equal to straights in January 2001.

ERASTES

This is kinda the ancient Greek name for a *Chicken Queen.*

EROMENOS

An' this is the ancient Greek name for a *Chicken*!

EUROVISION SONG CONTEST

The campest song contest in the whole wide world!

Who can forget Israel's **Dana International**, Russian fauxmo's *tatu*, Austria's gorgeous bearded drag diva **Conchita Wurst** an' the god-like **ABBA**!

But ma favourites were the three drag queens **Sestre** who sang **Samo Ljubezen** for Slovenia in 2002 – great outfits guys, shame y'all didn't win!

F

FTM

Female ta male, an' refers ta a guy that used ta be a gal, but went an' had a lil summat extra added.

FAG BANGLE

Straight gals seem ta lurve hangin' out with gay guys – Ah guess 'cause they're might fine company, an' add ta any gal's appearance.

FAG–HAG

Straight gal who likes ta hang out with gay guys.

FAGGOT

Slang term from the USA for gay fellahs. Originally abusive, but gay folk have reclaimed it (like **Queer**), which kinda takes the sting out. There's many suggestions as to why the word came ta mean what it does, including 'fagging' at Eton College, where a younger boy would be a servant to an older one, the bundles of sticks (known as 'faggots') that were used when guys were burned alive for bein' gay, an' ole word for a female prostitute, or it might'a come from *Feygeleh*. (See below.)

FAIRY

Gay guy, mainly 'cause some folk still reckon a gay guy has ta be all delicate and girly, which is just a crock'a crap

FAIRY LADY

Back in the 1900's folk assumed that gay gals were either big ole butches, or fluffy lil fairy ladies.

FALWELL, JERRY ☹

Ah can't figure out if this guy was crazier than a muskrat on prom night, or just plain mean, but he sure did hate gay folk!

On 10 February1999 his publication the *National Liberty Journal* published an article by *J.M. Smith* (a senior editor of the *NLJ*) sayin' that *Tinky Winky* of the BBC's kids TV show *Teletubbies* was a 'gay role model' 'cause he carries a purse, is purple (which, according to the *NLJ*, is the colour of "gay pride"), an' has a triangular antenna (which, also according to the *NLJ*, is the symbol of "gay pride"), an' 'cause'a all that is damaging ta the 'moral lives of children'.

But way worse is Jerry's following comment on the horrors of September 11th:

'I really believe that the pagans, and the abortionists, and the feminists, and the gays and the lesbians who are actively trying to make that an alternative lifestyle, the ACLU, people for the American way, all of them who have tried to secularize America. I point the finger in their face and say 'you helped this happen'

He then denied he'd ever said that, claimin':

'I would never blame any human being except the terrorists, and if I left that impression with gays or lesbians or anyone else, I apologize.'

Ah ain't sayin' no more, 'cause Ah'll just git nasty, an' anyhow ole Jerry done said "tubby bye-bye" on 15 May 2007, an' went on home ta the lord. Can y'all gimme "hallelujah"?

FAUXMOSEXUAL

This is a straight guy or gal who thinks it's cool ta pretend ta be gay or bi-sexual 'cause they think it'll make 'em more innerrestin', or even ta

51

git some other straight folk ta git down an' dirty with 'em!

FELCHING

Sex act where your lover comes in ya ass an' then sucks it all back out again. Not a safe-sex activity!

FELLATIO

Suckin' dick. Comes from the Latin word **fellare** (to be taken in the mouth)

FEMME

Girly-lookin' gay gal.

FEY

Camp gay guy. This is an ole French word for fairy.

FEYGELE

Originally meanin' 'lil bird' in Yiddish, this here's now used by Jewish folk ta mean a gay guy.

FIERSTEIN, HARVEY ☺

Harvey's a fabulous, talented gay guy!

Born on 6 June 1954 in Brooklyn, New York, he's an actor, writer, stand-up, drag queen, singer, an' is the winner'a four Tony awards.

His most famous movie, '**Torch Song Trilogy'**, came out in 1988, an' is based on his semi-autobiographical play of the same name.

He's also appeared in the movies **'Mrs Doubtfire'**, bin in the stage show **'Hairspray'** (starrin' in the role of Edna Turnblad, who was played by **Divine** in the movie), an' his version'a "**I am what I am**" in **La Cage aux Folles** dun brung me out in goose bumps. Harvey's even written a book called **'The Sissy Duckling'** for kids, which was made inta a HBO special in 1999.

FISH

Some older gay guys still refer ta gay gals as this, which goes ta show that it ain't just straight folk who use dumb an' offensive words!

Ah ain't goin' inta the why's an' wherefores' of what the word means 'cause y'all can figure it out for yaselves!

FISTING

Sex act where ya put ya fist in ya lover's ass or hoo-hoo.

FREEDOM FLAG AKA RAINBOW FLAG

Traditionally made of red, orange, yellow, green, blue and violet stripes (although the original also featured indigo and pink) the flag was first flown in San Francisco during the city's Freedom Day Parade in May 1978, an' was designed by **Gilbert Baker**.

The colours represent (in the order shown above): life, healing, sun, nature, art and spirit, with the lost indigo and pink symbolizin' harmony and sexuality respectively.

An' it proves we're all friends'a Dorothy!

FREEDOM RINGS

Lil ole bits'a jewellery in the colours of the freedom flag which were kinda popular in the early 1990s

FREE RIDE

A gay gal who likes ta receive, but not ta give (also known as a *'pillow princess'*.)

FRIEND OF DOROTHY

Slang term for a gay guy, 'cause'a the camp buddies who join Dorothy in *'The Wizard of Oz'*

FRONT MARRIAGE

Some unfortunate gay folk ain't allowed ta live life how they wanna, so have ta pretend ta be straight by gittin' hitched ta a guy or gal of the opposite sex. Ah think that's just a darn shame, for both'a 'em!

FROTTAGE

Comes from the French word for 'friction' an' it's when folk rub up against each other ta have sex instead'a stickin' anythang in.

G

GALPAL

Ah sure do lurve readin' that ole **National Enquirer**, an' this coy lil thang is their way'a sayin' one gal is gettin' all up close an' personal with another gal!

GATEWAYS CLUB

This lil ole club in King's Road, Chelsea, London, was *the* place ta be for gay gals from 1931 ta 1985. It even got ta be featured in the movies when some'a the **'The Killing of Sister George'** (see '**K**') was filmed there in 1968.

GAY

Comin' from an ole French word "**gai**" (meaning "happy"), this now pretty much means folk who hanker after folk of their own sex in that special kinda way, but it's reckoned that the word first got linked ta prostitutes an' straight folk who liked their pleasures ta be of a sexual nature in the 1880s (guess they thought workin' gals got a kick outta their jobs!), It didn't come to mean gay guys an' gals until the 1920s, when it was used by the writers **Noel Coward** (in the song '**Green Carnation'**) and **Gertrude Stein** (in her book '*Miss Furr and Miss Skeene'.)* - Ah guess both of 'em knew a few thangs about the subject, that's for sure!

In recent years, thanks ta the cartoon show **Southpark** (which Ah *do* lurve, despite maself!) some young'uns now use the word gay ta mean stuff that's useless or dumb, which rightly gets gay folk mighty riled.

GAY BASHING

Violent hate crime perpetrated on gay folk.

GAYBY

This here refers ta rug-rats bein' raised by two gay folk, an' comes from stickin' "gay" an" "baby" together.

GAY GAMES

This international athletic competition for gay folk is held every four years, an' was started by **Tom Waddell** in San Francisco (where else!) In 1982.

Tom, who came sixth in the decathlon in 1968's Mexico City Olympic games, wanted ta call them the gay Olympic games, but the United States Olympic Committee got all antsy an' filed a court action so's they couldn't use the 'O' word, an' tried ta git nearly 100,000 bucks in legal costs. The USOC (surely that should be 'U-SUC'?) weren't able ta git the money, but Tom wasn't allowed to use the word Olympic in the name.

Since they started, the games have been held all over the world, with the number of competitors growin' every year.

Sadly Tom died on 11 July 1987, but his fightin' spirit an' love of athletics lives on.

GAY MARRIAGE

Well butter ma butt an' call me a biscuit - on 29 March 2014 them ole Conservatives in the UK finally done let gay folk officially git wed, so y'all can now have the same rights as straight folk, plus y'all can git divorced too! Sadly folks in the US ain't quite as enlightened an' still cain't git wed in 31 States. Ma issue is just why in the heck cain't we jest call it "marriage", an' not have'ta stick "gay" or "same-sex" in front'a it?

GAY MEN'S CHORUS

Singin' group for gay guys, which began in San Francisco (what, another thang? Hat's off ta that city!) 0n 20 December 1978, the chorus has grown ta international status, with troupes in cities an' countries all over the world.

GAY NEWS/TIMES

This newspaper for gay guys was started in the UK, in 1972, by **Andrew Lumsden** an' **Denis Lemon**, an' they had a long history publishin' news an' fightin' dumb ole bigots (like that wicked ole witch **Mary Whitehouse**, who tried ta git 'em closed down 'cause of 'blasphemy').

The mag finally did go bust in 1983, but kinda got reborn in 1984 as **Gay Times**, which is now the best sellin' glossy mag for gay guys in the UK, an' part of the big ole publishin' an' retail chain **Millivres**, who also publish **Diva** for gay gals.

GAY PROM

In 1994 gay young'uns decided it was about time that they went ta the ball with the sweetie of their choice, an' not with some ole beard or handbag, so the **Lambda Youth Project** organised the first ever gay prom in Hayward, California, an' it's been goin' strong ever since.

GAY SWITCHBOARD

A phone service for gay guys an' gals (an' those who ain't sure yet!) with troubles, or who just wanta find out where the best bars are.

Most cities now have a switchboard that's there for y'all in times'a woe, so go check ya Yellerpages an' innernet.

GAY-IN

When gay pride parades first started in 1970 as a commemoration of the Stonewall Riots they went by a whole bunch'a different names, but San Francisco decided ta call theirs a gay-in, kinda like all'a them hippy 'love-ins' that were goin' on around about the same time.

GAYDAR

Some gay folk have an inbuilt way of tellin' if other folk are gay too, though it don't always work!

GAYS THE WORD

This store in Marchmont Street, London, has been providin' a good read for gay folk since January 1979, an' is still goin' strong, even though they got inta a heap'a trouble back in 1985 when UK customs tried ta prosecute 'em for sellin' books that the then government said where 'obscene an' indecent'.

Thankfully, most folk now realise that readin' a book ain't gonna turn ya gay if ya ain't, Ah mean, Ah've read **Betty Crocker**, but it sure didn't turn me inta a cook!

GENDER RE-ASSIGNMENT SURGERY

When a guy feels more like a gal, or a gal feels more like a guy, this is a big ole procedure ta sort thangs out an' make 'em feel happy with themselves, an' give 'em the body they really want ta have.

GLAAD

'Gay and Lesbian Alliance Against Defamation' formed in New York in 1985 ta protest the **New York Post**'s nasty, dumb writin' about AIDS,

An' GLAAD's been fightin' ever since then, protestin' an' raisin' awareness when-ever an' where-ever simple-minded bigots treat us an' our kind like crap.

GLASS CLOSET

Folk in this here closet reckon that they don't show that they're gay, when it's as obvious as a cherry on a cream pie ta everyone else around 'em!

GLORY HOLE

A lil ole hole in the wall in a men's bathroom that ya stick ya thang through for fun an' frivolity.

Glory be, just be careful where that thang end's up!

GODHATESFAGS ☹

Lord, Ah do declare, these folk are lower than the rent in a burnin' buildin'!

Formed as part'a **The Westboro Baptist Church** of Topeka, Kansas, this bunch is different from ya basic bunch'a shit-kickin' redneck dumb-asses 'cause they don't just spread their hate an' ignorance ta gay folk, but they also picket the funeral services'a military personnel 'cause they believe "**god has killed [the soldiers] in Iraq/Afghanistan in righteous judgment against an evil nation"**

Even though chief chowderhead an' leader **Fred Phelps** died on 19 March 2014 the minor members continue their hateful assholism.

Ah can't write no more about them, 'cause they make me sick ta ma stomach, but if y'all have stronger constitutions than ma own check out their web address at the end of the book – good luck!

GOLDEN HANDBAG AWARDS

This is a local lil ceremony that takes place in the *other* city by the sea, Brighton, in the UK, an' celebrates all that's great, good, an' gay friendly down there, like best eatin' place, sauna, club an what-not.

GOLDSTAR

This is a guy or a gal who ain't never got up close an' personal with a member'a the opposite sex.

GOOD VIBRATIONS

If ya like ta have ya fancy tickled (an' anywhere else for that matter!) then head ta this store in San Francisco! It's mainly for gay gals, thought it welcomes y'all, an' it sells all kinds'a fabulous toys that'll light up ya life an' put a big ole smile on ya face!

If ya can't visit in person ya can always buy stuff on the innernet, but if ya do git a chance ta drop by don't forget ta check out the scary ole vibrators from yester-year – yikes!

GREEK

Where would this here Lexicon be without the Greeks? There's a whole bunch'a words that come from the ancient Greek language, not ta mention all those Greek gay guys an' gals that have given so much ta us through history. 'Cause of all'a that some folk still refer ta anal sex as "goin' Greek"!

GREEN CARNATION

Back in 1894 a guy called **Robert Hitchens** wrote a short story called '*The Green Carnation*', which folk rightly guessed was about **Oscar wilde** (see '**W**' for lotsa info).

It weren't only 'cause the main characters were so close ta Oscar an' his main squeeze **Lord Alfred Douglas**, but 'cause'a the title itself, which was a flower that Oscar often wore in his lapel, an' which was reckoned ta be a secret sign for gay guys in Victorian times.

GROSS INDECENCY

In the UK this here is still what most gay guys git charged with if they're caught makin' whoopee in the great outdoors.

GUPPIES

Back in the 1980's some folk seemed ta git richer an' richer, an' got ta be known as yuppies (young urban professionals). Well, so's not ta be left out, rich gay folk got ta be known as *gay* urban professionals.

Ah ain't never been rich, so Ah guess Ah must be a puppie (poor, unprofessional person!)

GYM BUNNY

This here's a gay guy or gal who loves ta work out and spends the live long day pumpin' that ole iron.

GYNAEOTROPE

Kurt Hiller (see **Androtrope**) also wanted gay gals ta call themselves this, but as y'all probably realise (ya don't call yaself one, do ya?), that didn't catch on either

H

HALFORD, ROB ☺

Whatever ya musical tastes are (an' Ah confess Ah like a bit'a heavy metal maself) ya gotta give credit ta this guy.

Rob was the lead singer with British band *Judas Priest*, known for their hard rockin' music an' tough guy image, so imagine the shock that some folk got in 1998 when ole Rob came out (on a MTV rock show yet!). Way ta go!

HALL, RADCLYFFE

Born on 12 August 1880, ole Radclyffe (or John, as she liked ta be called) was a kinda messed up gal, who's best remembered for writin' *'The Well Of Loneliness'* in 1928, which ain't the cheeriest book about bein' gay ta ever come along, Ah can tell ya.

The book itself was banned in the UK, with *James Douglas* sayin' in the *Sunday Express* newspaper at the time that he'd sooner: '*give a healthy boy or a healthy girl a phial of prussic acid than this novel. Poison kills the body, but moral poison kills the soul.'* which Ah reckon is kinda harsh. They should'a read it, Ah reckon it could'a put most folk off bein' gay for life!

Anyhow, ole Radders had a pretty good time by all accounts. When she was 27 she shacked up with **Mabel Batten,** who was 50 at the time, an' when she croaked in 1915 Radclyffe got it together with Mabel's cousin, **Una Troubridge**.

The two gals were together until 1934, when Radclyffe got mighty friendly with **Evguenia Souline**, who was supposed ta be Una's nurse, but kinda showed a better bedside manner to Radclyffe, the sly ole dawg!

Radclyffe passed away on 7 October 1943, an' while she may not be much of a role model to us gay folk she's still an important part'a our history.

HANDBAG

If a gay guy has a beard as a fake straight date, then a gay gal has a handbag, which is a guy that pretends ta be her beau so folk don't find out she's gay.

HANKIES/BANDANNA

See the big ole list at the back - y'all find out all kinds'a innerestin' stuff!

HASBIAN

This is a gal who used ta be gay but now goes with guys. Comes from stickin' together "has been" an' "lesbian"

HEATHER HAS TWO MOMMIES

This lil ole kid's book by **Lesléa Newman** caused more fuss than a bucketful'a racoons when it came out in 1990. All those mad ole preachers got riled, an' said the book was 'anti-family', an' bad for the kiddie's morals an' the usual guff an' hoopla, an' it got taken off shelves all across the USA.
But thangs got real nasty in 1994 when two evil ole fools called **Robert Smith** an' **Jesse Helms** (both US senators at the time) got senate ta vote ta stop all federal fundin' for schools who: *'implement or carry out a program that has either the purpose or effect of encouraging or supporting homosexuality as a positive lifestyle alternative.'*

Ma next book is gonna be called *'Heather Has One Mommy An' An Asshole Stepdaddie Who Sits On The Couch All Day Drinkin' Beer',* an' Ah reckon it'll git all the fundin' it needs!

HEDWIG AND THE ANGRY INCH 🎬

This is another one'a ma favourite movies, with a mighty fine performance from **John Cameron Mitchell** as Hedwig, who starts out as a lil guy called Hansel growin' up in East Berlin, Germany before that nasty ole wall got torn down.

Hansel falls in lurve with the wrong guy, has a *really* bad experience on the operatin' table, an' spends the rest'a the movie as a gal called Hedwig, singin' some fantastic songs an' lookin' for real lurve an' happiness.

It'll make ya laugh, cry an' sing a-long.

HERNANDEZ, GILBERT & JAMIE ☺

Comic books again! These guys ain't gay, but they sure do have a lot of good gay stuff in their **Love and Rockets** comic books, an' all'a their gay characters are positive role models, an' never dumb ole stereotypes or nothin'.

An' on a personal note Ah reckon Jamie has written an' drawn the cutest, coolest lil gay gal ever, in the shape of **Esperanza Leticia Glass**, aka **Hopey**.

HETEROPHOBIC

Some gay folk just don't like straight folk, but this is usually 'cause the straight folk in question have acted like assholes.

HIDE THE CANDY

When a drag queen don't want the world ta know she's a he she tucks the goodies outta sight.

HIGH ENERGY

This here was *the* music for gay guys (an' gals) ta strut their stuff ta in the 1980's.

The main record label was **Record Shack**, an' most'a the tunes were created by songwriters **Ian Levine** an' **Fiachra Trench.**

It was a mixture of real fast disco an' camp euro-pop, an' high energy classics include '**So Many Men, So Little Time**' by **Miguel Brown**, an' o'course the anthem, '**High Energy**' by **Evelyn Thomas**

HIV

HIV stands for human immunodeficiency virus. HIV infects and gradually destroys an infected person's immune system, reducing their protection against infection and cancers.

Initially, someone living with HIV may show no symptoms of HIV infection as their immune system manages to control it. However, in most cases their immune system will need help from anti-hiv drugs to keep the HIV infection under control. These drugs do not completely rid the body of HIV infection.

(Ah took this directly from the Terence Higgins Trust website too: www.tht.org.uk)

HOMOPHILE

Back in the 1950s some gay folk didn't like the word 'homosexual', 'cause they figured it would make straight folk think that we only cared about what went on between the sheets, so they used this instead, 'cause "**phile**" comes from the Greek word for "love".

HOMOPHOBIA

Dumb an' sometimes violent hatred of gay folk.

HOMOPHOBIC

Folks who hate gay folk

HOMOSEXUAL

Gay guy or gal, thought the *homo* part is Latin an' literally means a guy, so Ah guess we gay gals should really call ourselves *'feminasexuals'*!

HOMOSEXUAL AGENDA

Oh ma lord, what will those dumb-assed fundamentalists come up with next! Lemme tell ya, they ain't fun, but they sure are mental!

Alan Sears an' *Craig Osten* of the *Alliance Defence Fund* came up with this here scare-story of a book in 2003.

Basically they reckon that we gay folk wanna stop people from treatin' us like crap (oh the horror!), but a'course they reckon we want their kids too, an' won't stop until the whole wide world is gay. Well, it'd sure be cleaner, an' the clothes would be *fabulous*!

Funnin' aside, these guys want'a drag us back ta the dark ages, where not only are we denied the right to git wed, we'd be denied jobs, housin', an' the basic human rights an' freedom that all folk should have, regardless of who they git it on with, or what they look like. These folk are mean an' evil, an' ya just gotta wonder what *their* agenda really is?

HOMOSEXUAL PANIC

Some straight guys just can't git ta grips with the idea that another guy could git the hots for 'em, an' git as jumpy as a long-tailed cat in a room full'a rockin' chairs (an' sometimes twice as nasty!)

Guys, quit actin' like jerks an' take it as a compliment, all y'all have ta do is say "no".

HUDSON, ROCK

Born on 17 November 1925 as **Roy Harold Scherer Jr**, Rock was a major movie star an' hunk in the 1950's an' 60's, with memorable leadin' roles, especially *'Pillow Talk'* an' *'Lover Come Back'*, with **Doris Day**.

He was a gay guy, though in those days major movie stars never told folk (not like today, huh, what d'ya mean....) an' sadly it wasn't until he got real sick with AIDS that the public knew.

He passed on 2 October 1985, an' his death, though a tragedy, did help to raise awareness of AIDS, an' show that anyone could be infected with this terrible disease.

HUNTLEYS

Boy howdy, this makes me chuckle!

Back in the 1950s when the folk cookin' up the **Wolfenden Report** had ta talk about gay guys an' workin' gals they didn't want ta shock the secretaries who had ta type up their findin's ('cause they were just gals, of course!) so they took ta referring to 'em as 'huntleys' (homosexuals) an' 'palmers' (prostitutes) – which is famous brand'a cookies in the UK!

HUSTLER

A guy (not always gay) who goes with other guys for money.

HYPOTHALAMUS

This here's part of ya brain, an' clever ole scientist **Simon Levay** reckoned in 1991 that gay guys have a bigger suprachiasmatic nucleus (which is responsible for lotsa bodily functions, includin' wantin' ta git it on) in theirs than straight guys do, which a lot of folk took ta mean that bein' gay ain't a choice, but part'a ya natural make up, which is a poke in the eye ta Jerry an' his bible-thumpin' buddies.

I

I.F.

This here mean's "intimate friend" an' it's what some gay folk like ta call their honey-buns.

IAN, JANIS ☺

Born on 7 April 1951 in New York, Janis is a cool, funky singer/song-writer, most famous for her sad ole song '*At Seventeen*'

Janis joined the ranks of the out an' proud in 1993, when she released the record '*Breaking Silence*', an album that nearly didn't git released until she put her own house up for sale ta finance it!

Ta date she's released over 30 record albums, an' also finds time ta write sci-fi books, an' tells some darn funny tales when she's on stage too!

IMMUNODEFICIENCY

This is when ya t-lymphocytes (helper t-cells) git killed off by HIV, an' ya body can't fight nasty infections, which means stuff that wouldn't normally be as bad ta other folk can make ya git real sick.

IMPORTUNING

When a gay guy takes a trip ta the cottage or tea room ta find a lil fun this is what folk might say he was doin'.
It comes from the Latin word **importūnus**, which means "bad", so Ah guess some meddlin' ole fool thought it up in the first place!

IN THE LIFE

Older gay guys an' gals use this ta mean bein' gay.

INGLE

This is an ole world meanin' a gay guy's sweetheart an' come's from the German word "**engel**", which means "angel" - ain't that sweet. However, some folk didn't think it *was,* so back in the 1700's it got ta mean a guy who went with other guys for money.

IN-HOUSE FRIEND

Some folk like ta be discreet about their significant others, so describe em' kinda coyly as this.

INTERNALISED HOMOPHOBIA

This is kinda sad. It's when gay folk don't wanna be gay, an' hate themselves for bein' that way. Folks, it ain't always easy, Ah know, but ya gotta be what makes ya happy, an' hidin' an' hatin' yourself ain't ever the way ta live!

INTERCRURAL SEX

From the Latin words for 'inside' an' 'legs' some gay guys do this here sex thang by rubbin' their dicks between their lovers thighs. It's kinda a safe-sex thang, but ya still gotta make sure that gloop don't go where it shouldn't.

INTERMEDIATE SEX

Folk are always comin' up with new words ta call us, but in 1908 **Edward Carpenter** (from the gay city'a Brighton no less!) came up with this here word for gay guys an' gals.

INTERSEXUALISM

Some folk used ta use this word ta describe gay fellahs, but that ain't strictly true, as it means someone who's born with the sexual bits'a both guys an' gals.

INVERT

Old term for gay folk, invented by **Sigmund** 'everyone really wants a dick' **Freud**

ISHERWOOD, CHRISTOPHER ☺

One'a ma favourite book-writers, Christopher was born on 26 August 1904 in High Lane, Cheshire, UK.

He wrote a whole bunch'a books, includin' '**The Berlin Stories**', which the world-famous movie '**Cabaret**' was based on (as well as the play '**I Am a Camera**'), '**Down There on a Visit**', an' '**A Single Man**', as well as a bunch'a books on travel an' eastern religion

Details of his life (moved to Berlin in 1928, travelled Europe, emigrated and settled in the USA in 1939) could fill a whole book on its own so Ah ain't gonna ramble on here, but will add that (of course!) he was a gay guy, who had a whole bunch'a romances, but eventually settled down with **Don Bachardy**, who he spent the last 33 years of his life with.

Armistead Maupin (see '**M**') told me that Isherwood was the biggest influence on his writin', an' his '**Tales Of The City**' series was directly inspired by '**The Berlin Stories**', an' ta ma mind there ain't no higher recommendation!

J

JAG HOUSE

This here's a special kinda house that's just chock full'a cute guys who all want'a give gay guys a good ole time – providing they pay for it of course – y'all know what Ah mean!

The word 'jag' is another way'a sayin' 'jerk', as in 'jerkin' off'

JAM

This here's a word that trendy young gay guys an' gals use for straight folk, an Ah guess it's 'cause there so darn many'a them, an' they're spreadin' all'a time! Funnin' aside, it actually stands for *j*ust *a* *m*an, 'cause they're simply so darned *ordinary*!

JEMIMAITE

It don't say nowhere that **Jemima Wilkinson**, who was born on 29 November 1752 in Rhode Island, USA, was a gay gal – in fact, she was an evangelist who preached ta all an' sundry about not havin' any kinda sex with anyone – but she was a rugged ole gal, given ta cuttin' down trees, ridin' around on a big ole horse, sayin' marriage was wrong, an' dressin' as a guy, so Ah'm gonna keep ma mind open about her sexuality!

Anyhow, gals in the 1800's who followed her teachin's were known as *Jemimaites*, an' Ah guess that can still apply to a whole bunch'a gals now-a-days too!

JENNY LIVES WITH ERIC AND MARTIN

Another lil book ta help young 'uns know that there's gay folk out there, this was written in 1981 by Danish straight (that's right!) gal *Susanne Bosche,* an' it caused a big ole shit-storm in the UK when it came out in 1983 an' young folk were readin' it in schools.

The then conservative government got on their high horse an' declared that the book was immoral, an' would lead ta the end of the world as we know it, an' they used it as part'a the reasonin' (Ah know that's the wrong word folk!) behind bringin' about Section 28

JERK-OFF PARTIES

Gay guys who care about bein' safe git together *an'* play together at these parties, where even if ya come last ya still have a mighty good time!

JETT, JOAN ☺

Born **Joan Marie Larkin** in Philadelphia on 22 September 1960, this gal formed the all-girl rock band **The Runaways** in Los Angeles in 1976, before startin' **The Blackhearts** in 1980, who she had the huge international hit '**I Love Rock & Roll'** with, an' has gone on ta have a successful career as both a rocker an' an actress.

She kinda 'officially' came out an' said she was a gay gal in **The Advocate** magazine in May 1994, an' has been known ta play a guitar with 'dykes rule' written on it, an' plays lotsa shows an' benefits for gay folk

An' on'a personal note, her version of '**Crimson and Clover'** really rocks ma world!

JETT-BLAKK, JOAN

This here ain't the same person as the gal listed above - Ah was mighty disappointed ta find out Ah wasn't gonna meet some cute rock-chick in black leather when Joan Jett-Blakk did a personal appearance at ma local book-store - but that's just 'cause Ah'm dumb an' didn't know no better at the time!
In fact this Joan is a really cool performer, political activist an' drag queen, who in 1992 ran for the presidency of the USA, as the **Queer Nation** party candidate. Sadly Joan

didn't win, an' instead we got some ole straight guy ta mis-manage the country as usual. Dang shame!

JOY OF GAY SEX

This here book by **Dr. Charles Silverstein** an' **Felice Picano** came out in the USA in 1977, an' was the first ta tell gay guys all there is ta know about the acts an' art of lurve.

JOY OF LESBIAN SEX

An' this one by **Emily L Sisley** an' **Bertha Harris** also came out in 1977, an' is just for the gals!

K

KAHLO, FRIDA ☺

Ah ain't really one for art an' the like, unless ya count the picture of dogs playin' cards hangin' in ma trailer, but Ah really cottoned ta this gal's paintings in a big way.

Magdalena Carmen Frieda Kahlo y Calderón was born on 6 July 1907 in Coyoacán, Mexico, an' had a tough ole life, ta say the least!

In 1913 she caught polio, which gave her trouble with her legs, an' in 1925 she nearly got killed when her bus was hit by a trolley car. After the accident she began paintin' ta help with the pain from her terrible injuries, an' the fact that she'd now never be able ta have kids.

Even though she was married ta **Diego Rivera** (who weren't no prize, lemme tell ya!), Frida never hid her bisexuality, an' carried on with lots'a gals, includin' the actress **Josephine Baker.**

KAPOSI'S SARCOMA AKA KS

KS is a form'a skin cancer, which can start all over the body, includin' the internal organs.

It attacks when the body's immunity has already been damaged, an' when folk git sick from HIV this can be one'a the main killers

KENRIC

This here organisation for gay gals gets its name from the areas of Kensington an' Richmond, in the UK, where it first started in November 1965.

They're still goin' strong today, an' provide fun, socializin' an' support for gay gals worldwide

KI KI

1940's slang term for a gay gal who weren't neither butch nor femme.

KILLING OF SISTER GEORGE

Ah personally don't like this movie, but it's one'a the first British films dealin' with gay gals, so Ah thought Ah'd better write a lil bit about it.

The movie came out in 1968, an' was based on the play of the same name by **Frank Marcus.**

It starred **Beryl Reid** as June Buckridge, an' **Susannah York** as Childie, June's main squeeze.

The two gals sure do have a twisted kinda lurve in this movie, both bein' real mean ta each other, an' at the end Childie gets down with June's biggest enemy Mercy Croft (played by **Coral Browne**) in what ta ma mind is one'a the scariest sex scenes ever filmed.

Ah think it's a nasty ole film, which kinda gives the impression that gay gals are spiteful, predatory booze-hounds an' sure think folk like **GLAAD** would have somethin' ta say if it was made today.

KING, BILLIE JEAN

Born on 22 November 1943 in Long Beach, Ca, Billie Jean is one'a the greatest tennis players ever, winnin' 37 grand slam tennis titles in total, 12 of those as a singles player.

She's also a gay gal, an' in 1981 she became the first US athlete ta come out.

She retired from playin' professional tennis in 1990, but is still very much involved in the game, an' does lots'a good work for gay causes an' charities.

KING, FLORENCE ☺

This gal is a grumpy ole puss, but Ah sure do lurve her writin'!

Born on 5 January 1936 in Washington DC Florence has written 11 books ta date, with ma favourite bein' *'Confessions of a Failed Southern Lady',* which details her younger life, an' is a real hoot!

She's also an out an' proud bisexual gal, who don't pull no punches or suffer no fools!

Ah kinda hope she never sees this as Ah'm sure she'd just *hate* it!

KINKY BOOTS

This first started out as a lil ole movie in 2005, set in Northampton, UK, an' told the true story'a Charlie Price (*Joel Edgerton*), a down on his luck boot factory owner who gets his fortune turned around when he teams up with the beautiful Lola/Simon (*Chiwetel Ejiofor*) ta make footwear for drag queens.

However, in 2013 the ever fabulous *Harvey Fierstein*, together with sassy chick *Cyndi Lauper*, done brung out a stage show in New

York City, which isn't just a mighty fine night out, but has also won a butt load'a awards (13 Tony nominations an' 6 wins ta date) Ah sure do lurve the show, thought Ah really think they gotta work on them Northamptonshire accents!

KINSEY REPORT

Dr Alfred C Kinsey wrote **Sexual Behaviour in the Human Male** in 1948, an' it was the first time anyone had writ anythin' so detailed on the subject, an' introduced the idea that 10% of all folk were gay, an' that 46% of all guys had been with another guy at one time or another.

He created a scale ta measure sexuality from one ta six, with six bein' someone who was totally gay.

The report was real important in both educatin' straight folk, an' also for givin' gay guys a chance ta see that they weren't the only one's out there.

KISS-IN

On 7 July 1987 a whole bunch'a gay folk (nearly 200!) got together in Piccadilly Circus, London ta protest Section 28 by kissin' an' generally bein' affectionate ta one an' other – make's ya proud ta have been part'a it!

KOROPHILE

This here's an older gay gal who like's young 'uns, an' it comes from the Greek words for gal (*koro*) an' lover (*phile).

L

L7 ☺

1990's all-girl rock band from California, these gals were gay-friendly, funny, feisty an' wrote some darn good songs, like '*Fast and Frightening*', with the lyrics:

Poppin' wheelies on her motorbike, straight girls wish they were dykes

They also appeared as 'Camel Lips' in the *John Waters* movie *'Serial Mom'*, and became infamous in the UK when singer *Donita Sparks* dropped her pants on the TV show *'The Word'*, an' threw her used tampon at the mud-slingin' audience at *The Reading Music Festival* in 1991

In 2006 Donita (an' other famous folk) got asked ta shoot a roll'a film as part of a charity event, which was auctioned on eBay, an' all'a the cash went ta film group *MIX NYC*, run by an' for gay folk in New York.

L-FEST

Durin' the third weekend in July in Uttoxeter Racecourse, Staff, UK is overrun (but in a good day!) with gay gals, all celebratin' and groovin' at L-Fest, a festival'a comedy, music, and general happy goin's on.

Started in 2010 by **Cindy Edwards** this is THE place for a gay gals ta go – as long as she don't mind livin' in a tent for the weekend. Ah gotta admit, Ah ain't never been, mainly 'cause Ah'm the kinda gal that likes ta sleep in a bed, but many'a ma good buddies have, an' they say it's a blast! Now, where can Ah get a leopard print sleepin' bag...?

L WORD

This here show, which came out in 2004 an' ran for 6 season, was the first soap for gay gals, an' was about'a buncha beautiful, rich gals an' their beautiful, rich buddies in LA.

It was made by **ShowTime**, created by **Ilene Chaiken**, an' directed by **Rose Troche**, who made the movie '**Go Fish'**, an' was a refreshin' change from watchin' stories about the goin's on'a straight folk, thought Ah'd say there was a lil too much boy/gal sex in the first season, but they soon stopped all that foolishness in the followin' seasons.

LABYRIS

This was said ta be one'a the weapons used by those Amazon gals, an' it's a big ole double-headed axe.

Gay gals adopted this as one'a their symbols, an' ya used ta see jewellery an' stuffed based on it all over, but it's kinda lost its popularity in recent times.

LADY GAGA ☺

This gal may have only been around for a couple'a years or so, but boy, she's sure created a stir! Born *Stefani Joanne Angelina Germanotta* in **NYC on** March 28, 1986, she not only makes mighty fine music, but is a huge supporter of gay folk and their rights, an' has been totally open about bein' bisexual.

At the time'a writin' she's release 3 studio albums, but sold 27 million copies'a 'em, and Ah'd say she's fixin' ta be around for a long ole time.

LAMBDA

After the gay folk rebelled at the Stonewall Inn in 1969 *Tom Doerr* of the *Gay Activist*

Alliance of New York City suggested that this be used as a symbol for gay folk everywhere.

It's the eleventh letter in the Greek alphabet an' was used ta show kinetic potential, unity an' knowledge.

There's now a bunch'a folk who use the name as part'a their identity, includin' *Lambda*, who help folk who suffer due ta homophobia, *Lambda Literary,* for lgbt readers and writers, an' *Lambda Legal*, who've been fightin' for the rights'a gay folk since 1973.

lang, k.d.

Born *Kathryn Dawn Lang* on 2 November 1961 in Alberta, Canada, k.d's probably one'a the most famous gay gals ta come along for a long while.

Ta date she's released 14 record albums, won a bunch'a Grammies, an' starred in the movie '*Salmonberries*' in 1993. She's also a vocal supporter'a animal rights an' vegetarianism, as well as bein' a big ole role model for gay gals.

LATENT

When someone ain't quite figured out if they're gay or not yet.

LAVENDER

This here colour is traditionally associated with gay folk, with bein' gay known as livin' a 'lavender lifestyle'. Ah guess it's 'cause the colour is kinda easy on the eye, an' is nice an' festive too – Ah sure do lurve it!

LAVENDER MARRIAGE

When a closeted gay gal an' guy decide ta tie the knot ta fool folk inta thinkin' they're straight

LEATHERMAN/WOMAN

Kinda speaks for itself, this is a guy or gal who likes ta slap on a lil bit'a cow-hide, from leather pants ta a cute lil biker hat or more!

LEFT HANDEDNESS

Uneducated folk have long reckoned that usin' yer left hand is a sign'a bein' odd (if not downright sinister – blame the ancient Romans for that foolishness), but also that a guy or gal is more likely ta be gay if'n they's a south paw.

Most folk used ta reckoned that this thinkin' was dumber than a box'a hair, but studies back in 2003 seemed ta show that some'a the guys they looked at were 31% more likely ta be gay, an' a big ole 91% of the leftie gals turned out ta be lesbians!

Ah don't know if any'a this is strictly scientific, but it sure is innerrestin', especially as Ah maself am a southpaw!

LESBIAN

A gay gal. It gets its name from folk who live on the lil ole island **Lesbos** in Greece.

LESBIAN BED-DEATH

When two gay gals have been together for a long time for some reason they git kinda tired of gettin' jiggy all'a time, an' end up more as regular room-mates than the sexual kind, which is sorta sad.

LESBIAN FEMINIST

These gals ain't quite as extreme as the separatists below, they just believe that women have a tough ole time 'cause'a guys, an' wanna make sure we ain't treated like dirt an' git all that's due to us in the way'a jobs, pay an' what-not, which is how it should be!

LESBIAN SEPARATIST

Back in the 70s an' 80s there were gay gals who had a real problem relatin' ta guys, either straight or gay, so they chose not ta hang out with any of 'em, an' tried to live totally separate lives. It's a kinda innerrestin' idea, but sure makes it hard ta buy groceries an' stuff!

LESBOS

Pronounced 'Lesvos' this here island in Greece was where the Greek poetess *Sappho* (see '*S*' for more info) hung out an' taught gals all kinds'a mind expandin' thangs, which is the reason that gay gals today are mostly known as lesbians.

It's also a darn beautiful place ta visit, providin' y'all take ya hikin' boots – why are all gay places so danged hilly?

LBGT

Folk don't like ta be left out, so now-a-days a bunch'a queers are known as 'lesbian, bisexual, gay and transgender'.

LICK BOX

Gay guys used ta be called this at the start'a the 1900s, but Ah'll be darned if Ah can figure out why!

LIPSTICK-LESBIAN

Another name for **femme**, first used in the 1980's.

LONGTIME COMPANION

Back in the 80s when gay guys started getting' sick an' dyin' of aids the folk who ran the newspapers didn't like ta put that other guys were their next'a kin in obituaries, so they used this phrase instead'a 'lover' or somethin' more intimate.

LORDE, AUDRE

Born on 18 February 1934 in Harlem, New York Audre was a gay gal who wrote over 12 books'a poetry, dealin; with her life as, she stated, a **black lesbian, mother, warrior, poet**.

Sadly she passed away on 17 November 1992 after a 14 year battle with cancer, but remains one'a the greatest writers of poetry for folk, be they black, gay or otherwise.

LOVE THAT DARE NOT SPEAK ITS NAME (THE)

Oscar Wilde came up with this here term ta describe gay folk, back when they weren't allowed ta talk about it.

It was also an infamous poem by **James Kirkup** (see '**Whitehouse, Mary'** for more info)

LOW FEMME

A gay gal who ain't butch, an' prefers ta look a lil girly, but is still happy ta kick it in jeans (as long as she's got a purse an' matchin' high heels of course!)

LUBE

This here goo makes getting' inta tight places way easier, thought remember guys an' gals, if ya use it with a condom it's gotta be water-based so's not ta damage the latex.

The word itself is an abbreviation of lubricant, but Ah figure y'all knew that anyhow!

LUG

Lesbian until graduation - meanin' them straight gals that like ta "experiment" in college.

LYON, PHYLLIS ANN

This good ole gay gal was born on 10 November, 1924 in Tulsa, Oklahoma an' was a force ta be reckoned with in the gay rights movement.

Together with her long-time honey **Del Martin** (who she met in 1950, an' was still goin' strong with until Del's passin' on August 27, 2008), Phyllis formed the **Daughters Of Bilitis** in 1955, ta give other gay gals a chance ta meet one an' other an' fight against oppression.

In 1967 the two gals joined the **National Organisation For Women**, an' got 'em ta be a lil more open ta gay gals, an' in 1989 they got involved in **Old Lesbians Organizing For Change**, ta git more rights for long-in-the- tooth gay gals

M

MTF

Meanin' 'male ta female', this is a gal that used ta be a guy

MACONDRAY LANE

This lil ole lane in San Francisco is where Armistead Maupin (see below) got the idea for Barbary Lane. It ain't strictly gay a'course, but its well worth a visit if y'all are in town, just ta say ya've been there, but remember ta bring ya hikin' boots, as its way up a scary ole hill!

MADONNA

She might be queen'a the fauxmo's, but this gal has done heaps ta git folk innerrested in sex, both straight an' gay.

On **The Letterman Show** back in 1988 she got folk guessin' as ta whether or not she was doin' the do with **Sandra Bernhard**, she showed gals gittin' it on together in the video for '**Justify My Love'** in 1990, an' then in 2003 she made the headlines again by plantin' a big ole smacker on **Britney Spears** at the **MTV Video Music Awards**.

Some folk might say she does all'a this stuff 'cause she's kinda desperate ta stay in the limelight an' all, but Ah say 'gal, if it makes folk realise the whole world ain't straight then go right on ahead!' – not that she'd give a goddamn hoot what Ah think!

MANCHESTER

This here town is the gayest in the north'a England, with most'a the action goin' on in Canal Street.

The area got real famous when much'a '**Queer as Folk'** (the original UK version) was filmed there in 1999, an' they have one'a the best Prides in the UK.

MARY

Older gay guys sometimes refer ta each other as 'Mary', an' folk think it may come from the word **maricón,** which ain't a nice word that Spanish-speakin' folk use for gay guys

MATTACHINE SOCIETY

A gay guy named **Harry Hay** started this group for other gay guys in Los Angeles on 11 November 1950.

It was named for the 16th century French musical masked singin' group the **Société Mattachine**, as Harry felt that gay folk had ta wear masks ta hide the way they were. He wanted ta show that; *'physiological and psychological handicaps need be no deterrent in integrating 10 percent of the world's population towards the constructive social progress of mankind'*, which is both kinda wordy an' kinda negative, but Ah guess his intentions were good!

The society formed groups all over the USA, an' although its old-fashioned ways kinda lost favour after the gay rebellion at *The Stonewall Bar*, it carried on until 1987, when it finally closed.

MAUPIN, ARMISTEAD ☺

Born on 13 May 1944, in Washington DC Armistead is one'a the best writers for gay folk ta ever come along.

He's best known for the *'Tales of the City'* series'a books (there's nine in all at the time'a writin'), which detail the lives of the folk livin' in the fictional Barbary Lane in San Francisco. There's gay guys an' gals, straight one's, one that used ta be a guy an' then became a gal (Ah ain't sayin' who in case y'all haven't read 'em yet!), an' another guy who used ta be a gal – he's got the whole beautiful rainbow in there!

He's also written two other books, '**Maybe the Moon**', an' '**The Night Listener**', an' a short called '**Jackie Old**', about Jackie Kennedy, an' even done developed "**Tales**" in'ta musical show!

Apart from bein' a writer Armistead does a lot'a good work raisin' awareness of the struggles of gay folk, an' those livin' with HIV an' AIDS, an' is a campaigner ta git those sad ole closeted celebrities ta git real an' come on out!

MEAT GAZERS

These gay guys like ta see what's on offer in their local cottage or tearoom – just be sure he ain't hidin' a badge boys!

METROPOLITAN COMMUNITY CHURCH

Ah ain't one for church-goin', Ah have ta confess, but if y'all are, this is the place ta go!

Back in 6 October 1968, in Huntington Park, California, USA, reverend **Troy Perry** got a bunch'a folk together an' started Christian church services for gay folk, who sure weren't gittin' any support from the regular Christian church!

The MCC now has congregations in over 22 countries, an' provide all kinds'a spiritual help for gay folk the world over.

METROSEXUAL

This was first used back in the 90s ta describe straight guys who didn't like ta git it on with other guys, but liked ta take care'a how they looked an' smelled an' stuff, which, let's face it, all folk should do, an' it shouldn't have any ole thang ta do with who they cotton ta!

MICHIGAN WOMYN'S MUSIC FESTIVAL

Since it started in the 1970s this lil ole music show has been attractin' gay (an' straight) gals who wanta play an' hear music, free from a bunch'a guys askin' ta see their boobs an' generally bein' assholes!

Folk kinda have the opinion that its full'a hairy-pitted veggies, who pray ta the moon-goddess an' don't hardly wash, but they're just ignorant. Ah'm sure livin' in a tent for two weeks in August an' listenin' ta sensitive, acoustic based music is a very healin', spiritual thang ta do.

MILK, HARVEY

Born on 22 May 1930 in New York, Harvey moved ta San Francisco in 1972, an' got real involved in politics, an' became known as '*The Mayor of Castro Street*'

In 1977 he was the first openly gay guy ta be elected city supervisor, a position he used ta fight for the rights of gay folk in the city.

Sadly on 27 November 1978 **Dan White**, a former city supervisor who disagreed with Harvey's gay rights bill, shot an' killed both Harvey an' the mayor, **George Moscone**.

After White got a sentence of only seven years an' eight months the gay folk in the city rightfully went nuts, in what was ta become known as the **'White Night Riot'**.(see '**W**'.)

A movie was made about his life in 2008, starrin' **Sean Penn** as Harvey, an' directed by **Gus van Sant,** which Sean even bagged a best actor Oscar for.

MILLIVRES

This UK based gay company first started in 1974, an' are now *the* force ta be reckoned with as a gay business, publishin' nearly all'a the gay magazines available in the UK (includin' '**Diva**', '**Gay Times**' an' '**The Pink Paper**'), an' a whole load'a books, an' ownin' the '**Prowler**' chain'a stores

MINCE

Some camp gay guys walk with lil bitty steps, but be warned if ya say it folk, this here word comes from the Book'a Isaiah in *The Bible*, an' the full reference is:

'*Moreover the lord saith, because the daughters of Zion are haughty, and walk with stretched forth necks and wanton eyes, walking and mincing as they go: therefore the lord will smite with a scab the crown of the head of the daughters of Zion'* (3:16-18)

So it ain't exactly nice!

MISSIONARY WORK

Not ta be confused with meddlin' Christian folk, this is when a gay guy or gal tries ta "convert" straight folk (in ma mind it's a waste'a time, but hey if y'all hanker for a heap'a trouble go to it!)

MOLLY HOUSES

Back in the 1700s these were bars where workin' gay guys (known as '*mollies*') went ta dress as gals, meet each other an' generally have a grand ole time.

MUSCLE MARY

A gay guy who likes ta work out at the gym a lil bit too much.

MUTUAL MASTURBATION

This is when y'all play nicely with each other – it's fun, an' it's safe too!

N

NAFF

Ah ain't gonna list a whole bunch'a Polari words in this here Lexicon, 'cause other folk have done that already, but this here word used ta mean straight folk (some folk reckon it stood for "*n*ot *a*vailable *f*or *f*uckin'), an' is now used in everyday UK language ta mean summat that's kinda crappy. Hmmm...

NAIL CLIPPERS

Every gay gal should have a set'a these thangs (unless she's a pillow princess!) as it just ain't right ta go at ya best gal with a scary ole set'a claws!

NAMES FOUNDATION PROJECT

This here quote is from the names foundation website an' says it better than Ah could:

Founded in 1987, the Aids Memorial Quilt is a poignant memorial, a powerful tool for use in preventing new HIV infections, and the

largest ongoing community arts project in the world.

Each "block" (or section) of the Aids Memorial Quilt measures approximately twelve feet square, and a typical block consists of eight individual three foot by six foot panels sewn together. Virtually every one of the more than 40,000 colorful panels that make up the quilt memorializes the life of a person lost to AIDS.

Ah got ta see some of it on vacation in San Francisco, an' it brung more than a few tears to ma eyes, an' Ah dearly hope there comes a time when they stop addin' to it, an' we cure this terrible disease

NANCY BOY

Lil ole term for a girly-actin' gay guy.

Folk reckon this comes from the actress **Anna Oldfield** (born 1683, an' died 1730), who got ta be known as 'Miss Nancy' 'cause she was such a darn fancy-pants, an' right purdy ta boot.

NATURE OR NURTURE?

Folk still can't seem ta agree if gay guys an' gals are made that way or not, an' this here term refers ta that lil ole quandary.

Of course, ya git the bible-thumpers who reckon folk are turned gay by books an' TV an' the like, but the more rationally minded have figured out that it don't just happen like that, folk are born gay, but mayhap they need a lil time ta find out what's right for 'em.

An' it ain't just folk, there's plenty'a other critters that are gay, like the penguins **Silo** an' **Roy** in **Central Park Zoo**, New York, who have been a lurvin' couple for eight years ta date, an' have even raised a young 'un called **Tango**, despite both bein' male! This ain't a one off thang with penguins it seems, cos in Kent, UK two other guy birds **Jumbs** and **Kermit** are doin' the same thang.

NAVRATILOVA, MARTINA

Do gay gals play better tennis than straight ones? Ah can't say for definite, but this one sure seems ta!

Born on 18 October 1956, in Czechoslovakia, Martina defected an' became a citizen of the USA in 1981, an' became the biggest female racket-swinger in the world, winnin' 58 grand-slam titles in all, 18'a them as a singles player, an' won the Wimbledon tournament 9 times.

She came out as a gay gal in 1981, an' even though her choices of gal-pals ain't been that hot (**Rita Mae Brown** for one, not ta mention

109

ole *Judy* 'hand me ya wallet' *Nelson*!), Martina has been a huge inspiration ta gay an' sporty gals the world over. An' she's a south-paw ta boot!

NELLIE/NELLY

This here's yet another name for a girly actin' gay guy, an' like most others, it don't come with much of a nice history, even though gay folk have now reclaimed it.

Some folk reckon it's taken from the Cockney rhymin' slang phrase *Nelly Duff*, which was used ta mean 'puff' (see *pouffe*) back in the 1940's, though others say it comes from the sweet ole song "*Nellie Dean*", made popular by British music hall singer *Gertie Gitana* in the 1900s, which in turn got ta be rhymin' slang for "queen"

NON-OP(ERATIVE)

These are trans folk who live as the opposite sex but who ain't had no surgery.

NO OUTSIDERS PROJECT

Lordy, this kinda shows how far we've come, as this piece'a legislation that started in 2007 in the UK is ta teach kids it's ok ta be different, an' that folk should be treated equal, no matter who they like ta bunk with!

They use a bunch'a books ta show kids that they're not freaks, includin' books about gay critters, an' about other kinds'a families that folk can have, an' even take steps ta stop gay kids from bein' bullied. It's a dang long way from Section 28, an Ah for one think it's a fantastic piece'a progress!

O

O'BRIEN, RICHARD ☺

Born **Richard Smith** on 25 March 1942 in Gloucester, England, Richard's best known for writin' the fantastic '**Rocky Horror Picture Show**", which started out as a stage show in 1973, an' then became a cult movie in 1975, influencin' music an' the way folk dressed forever after.

Richard don't like ta be 'labelled' in what he does in bed, but he sure is gay-friendly, an' also hosts an annual show called **Transfandango** for 'trans 'n' gentle people' which raises money for the **Royal Manchester Children's Hospital**, so Ah guess he ain't just talented, he's an all-round good guy too!

O'DOWD, GEORGE ☺

Born on 14 June 1961 in London, England this lil ole gay guy has had more ups 'n down's than a polecat on a trampoline, that's for sure!

He first found fame as **Boy George** in the 80s with **Culture Club**, who had a string'a hit records, like **'Do You Really Want to Hurt Me'**, an' the world-wide smash hit *'Karma Chameleon'*

But despite the hits it weren't too rosy in the Culture Club camp, as George was havin' a lurve thang with drummer *Jon Moss,* who it turned out weren't too comfortable about bein' with another guy (well, almost...) an' didn't treat George too good mosta the time.

Unfortunately George got a lil too innerrested in recreational drugs, includin' heroin, which led ta Culture Club breakin' up in 1986. Thankfully he had folk lookin' out for him, an' his brother *David O'Dowd* went on ta British television ta tell the world about George's drug problem an' ta beg him ta git help (Ah guess he didn't have no telephone at the time!), which kinda vexed George, but combined with some'a his buddies dying cause'a the drug, an' being arrested, made him git the help he needed.

George moved on ta bein' a club dj, a successful solo singer, a musical writer (*'Taboo'*, based on his life), as well as writin' two fantastic autobiographies, *'Take It Like A Man'*, an' *'Straight'*, an' has even done a buncha shows with the re-formed *Culture Club*.

But he got hisself inta another heap of trouble in 2008 when he got convicted'a assaultin' an' imprisonin' *Audun Carlsen*, an' got sentenced ta fifteen month in jail (though he got out after four) - hon, Ah dunno if y'all will ever see this, but y'all are too talented for all this foolin' about, an' Ah for one hope y'all will be a good boy from now on!

OFF OUR BACKS

First published on 27 February 1970 in Washington DC, USA this is a lil ole mag for gay gals who like ta put a bit'a politics in their sex-lives.

The mag has gone from strength ta strength, an' ta date is the longest runnin' feminist mag in the USA

OKAMA

This is the Japanese word for a gay guy, an' it comes from an ole word for "butt", so Ah guess y'all can see what they all thought about gay guys!

OKOGE

This here is the Japanese word for "fag hag", an' literally translates ta ""burnt rice stickin' ta the bottom of'a cook pot", so Ah also guess they didn't think much of these gals in Japan!

114

OLD HORATIAN WAY

Charles Skinner Matthews (a buddy'a ***Lord Byron***, who weren't no stranger ta the way!) is said ta have come up with this as code for gay goin's on in the 1800s

He an' ***Byron*** wrote a heap'a letters ta each other about their sexual shenanigans, but 'cause two guys bein' together was illegal they used ta refer ta the ancient poet ***Horace***, who is said ta have trod the way plenty'a times himself!

OLIVIA

Since 1973 (when it started out as a record label!) Olivia has been sendin' gay gals on vacations around the whole wide world!

They do a whole bunch'a cruises, which feature all kinds'a entertainment, from dance parties, celebrity performers, an' fun an' games, they have special resorts where gay gals can have a good ole time an' not have ta fret about gittin' any hassle, an' have now got 'emselves a website that offers news, datin' an' all kinds'a information for gay gals with a thirst for knowledge an' adventure – go check 'em out!

OMNISEXUAL

This here's another word for guys an' girls that like both guys an' girls!

ON OUR BACKS

Started in 1984 by gay gals **Nan Kinney** an' **Debi Sundahl** this here mag was for gals who wanted ta put a *lot* of sex in their lives! It was a reaction ta what the gals thought was the kinda priggish attitude ta sex in *Off Our Backs* (see above) an' was chock full'a all kinds'a comin's an' goin's, by an' for sexy ole gay gals everywhere!

Sadly the mag died a death in 2006, but y'all can still check out their web-site ta git yaselves all hot an' bothered!

ONE MAGAZINE

One'a the first mags for gay guys, **One** was founded in 1952 in LA, USA, by the **Mattachine Society** (see '**M**'), as a mag ta show that folks could be proud'a bein' gay, an' of course, those Christian creeps got inta a big ole stew over that!

In October 1954 they got the Postal Service all riled up too, who refused ta handle that month's issue of the mag, as they said it was *"obscene, lewd, lascivious and filthy,"* (heck, so's *The National Enquirer*!) but the folk at *One* went all the way ta the Supreme Court, an' on 13 January 1958 they won a landmark case, so's all gay mags could be sent through the mail legally, an' without the Postal Service getting' all uppity about it. Way ta go, *One*!

OPERATION SPANNER

Back in December 1990 a bunch'a gay guys in Manchester, England got inta a heap'a trouble 'cause'a the thangs they liked ta do with each other in the name'a havin' a good time.
This was 'cause the police found'a video tape in 1987 showin' the guys doin' all manner'a thangs ta each other (includin' sandpaperin' each other balls, and lots'a cuttin'), and figured it for a snuff movie.

The guys all got hauled inta court, an' some'a 'em got jail sentences for upta three years.

It were finally decided in 1995 – thanks ta campaign group '*Countdown On Spanner*' - that if folk wanted ta do this kinda stuff ta each other it was up to them, an' the guys got their convictions over-turned, an' folk started ta fight for the rights'a the SM community (both gay an' straight)

ORANGE IS THE NEW BLACK

Ah came ta this show a lil late, but tie me down an' tickle me is it good! Set in the fictional Litchfield Women's Penitentiary, it's based on **Piper Kerman's** true life experiences, an' tells the story'a her time in prison. It's funny, thought-provokin' an' sexy as the dickens, starrin' **Taylor Schilling** as Piper, an' **Laura Prepon** as her ex squeeze Alex. The show also stars **Lea Delaria** an' **Natasha Lyonne** (from "**But I'm a Cheerleader**"), as well as a whole mess'a other great talent. Ah cain't recommend it enough!

ORTON, JOE ☺

Born 1 January, 1933, in Leicester, England, this lil gay guy was one'a the most talented play-writes ta come out'a the UK.

He wrote a bunch'a real funny – an' kinda sick - stuff, including '**Loot**', '**Entertaining Mr Sloan**' an' '**What the Butler Saw**', all dealin' with the worst parts'a human nature, but in a real comical way.

He had'a long term thang with fellow writer **Kenneth Halliwell**, (who had a few problems with depression), an' as the years went on Ken started ta feel second place, 'cause'a Joe's success, an' his constant playin' around, an' tragically on 9 August 1967 Ken hit Joe upside the head with a hammer a whole bunch'a times, killin' him, an' then took a bucket-load'a pills an' killed himself.

If y'all wanta know more check out the plays above, read the book '*Prick Up Your Ears*' by *John Lahr,* (or rent the real good movie'a the same name, starrin' *Gary Oldman* as Joe and *Alfred Molina* as Kenneth), which tells the full story.

In 2009, some lucky folk in the UK got ta go see a play based on the book an' movie, starring "only gay in the village" *Matt Lucas* as Kenneth Halliwell, but this sadly closed early cause Matt had some personal tragedy when his ex-husband *Kevin McGee* done killed hisself.

OTTER

This here is a term for a young feller who likes ta party with bears, but who ain't big or hairy hisself.

OUT ON TUESDAY

Back on 14 February 1989 Channel 4 on British TV gave us a Valentine's Day ta remember when they broadcasted the first ever TV show just for gay guys an' gals – an' anyone else who might'a been innerested!

119

The first series had eight episodes, coverin' all kinds'a thangs, from comin' out ta goin' out, an' thangs got even better on 6 march 1990, when they brung out a further ten episodes.

OUTING

Some folk don't think that anyone should be in the closet, an' will do their darndest ta make sure everyone knows that other folk are gay.

Ah reckon this is kinda cool in principle, but also think that folk should be given the right ta say so when they're good an' ready, rather than havin' ta admit ta it like it's some dirty lil secret – but that still don't stop me buyin' *The National Enquirer* ta see who they're haulin' outta the closet!

P

PDA

This here stands for '**public display of affection**', an' some straight folk still can't stand it if gay guys or gals kiss an' hug each other outside'a their trailers! Git real, folk, we ain't hurtin' no-one!

PACKING

Some butch gay gals like ta play at bein' guys, an' this is when they shove a lil (or big!) ole somethin' down their pants ta make it look like they've got a dick!

PANSY

Yet another nasty ole term for a gay guy! This here comes from Elizabethan days when gay guys were considered delicate an' girly (an'a course, lavender!)

PARKS, ALEX

Born 26 July 1984 in Cornwall, England, this gal was the first out gay gal ta win the BBC TV music contest *Fame Academy* in 2003.

She went on ta have a couple'a hit records called '**Maybe That's What It Takes**', '**Cry**', an' '**Looking for Water**', before kinda disappearin' again.

PASSIVE

Folk who like ta have stuff done ta them in the bedroom, but ain't too innerested in doin' much in return.

PEDERASTY

This is when a younger gay guy an' an older one reach a state'a mutual respect an' meetin'a the minds (an' other body parts!) - an' once again it's a word that comes from those ole Greeks, with '**ped**' meanin' '**young'un**' and '**eros**' meanin' '**lover**'.

PERRY, KATY

Now, Ah took against this gal cause'a her big hit "**I Kissed A Girl**", which kinda sticks in ma craw, 'cause ta me she seems ta treat bein' a lesbian as a bit'a fooling around, but Ah know that a lotta gay gals seem ta like it, an' she's done some cool stuff for AIDS charities, so Ah guess Ah'm gonna cut her some slack!

PERRY, LINDA ☺

Born on 15 April, 1965, in Massachusetts, USA this fantastic out gay gal is one'a my favourite singer/songwriters.

She first got famous as the lead singer of (kinda) out dyke band *4 Non-Blondes*, pennin' the world-wide hit record *'What's Up?*" in 1993, but after leavin' the band, an' having a couple'a solo albums ('*In Flight* ' an' '*After Hours*'), kinda got fed up with the lime-light, an' took ta writin' a bunch'a hit records for other folk, includin' "*Get The Party Started*" for *Pink* (in 2001), "*Beautiful*" for *Christina Aguilera* (in 2002), an' "*What You Waiting For?*" with *Gwen Stefani* (in 2004), all'a which are good ole songs, but Ah kinda wish she'd take ta singin' herself again, 'cause none'a them gals hold a candle ta her in the hollerin' department!

For me worlds kinda collided when Ah heard that she'd done wed *Sara Gilbert*, who played Darlene in the TV show *Roseanne*, on 30 March 2014 – congratulations gals!

PHILAENIS

Another ole Greek, this gal lived in Samos durin' the 4th century BC, an' is said ta have

123

writ a book all about lurvin' guys an' gals –
which accordin' ta history she sure did put a
lot'a research inta!

PILLOW PRINCESS

Usually a gay gal (thought Ah guess guys do it
too!) who just likes ta lay there an' git all the
good stuff, without givin' none of it back – not in
ma trailer honey!

PINK NARCISSUS

These boys are a real cool alternative rock
band, who make their home in Brighton, UK.

Ah'd have liked their music anyhow, but Ah'm
even more partial to 'em cos they done gave
me ma actin' debut in their video for
"*Disinfectant*", and Ah also got ta dance
around in the video for "*Masquerade*".

Lead singer *Oli Spleen* also hosts a weekly
club night called *Fag Machine*, which ain't for
the uptight or faint-hearted!

PINK PAPER

This free newspaper for gay guys an' gals
started in 1987, in London, UK, but sadly bit the
dust in September 2012, though they still got a
datin' website.

PINK POUND/PINK DOLLAR

When businesses cottoned on ta the fact that gay folk like ta shop they started providin' a whole bunch'a goodies that we can spend our hard earned money on, from greetin' cards ta vacations.

PINK SQUIRREL

This here's ma tipple'a choice, an' here's the recipe:

1 part crème de cacao
1 part crème de noyaux
1 part heavy cream
shake with crushed ice. Strain into a chilled glass

They're not strictly gay, but they sure are good!

PINK TRIANGLE

Symbol used in Nazi concentration camps ta identify gay guys.

POLARI

Back in the UK in the 1950s guys still got sent ta jail for being gay, so they came up with a way'a speakin' in code so's folk didn't realise what they were talkin' about.

The language was taken from a bunch'a Italian words (*Polari* itself comin' from the Italian word '*parlare*', meanin' '*ta talk*'), an' English words said backwards, includin' stuff like '*riah*' for hair, and '*bona ecaf*' for 'he sure is cute'.

Once the law changed in 1967 gay guys didn't need ta be so secretive, but some folk still use it today, an' a whole bunch'a words - like *blag* (ta git somethin') an' *slap* (make-up) - ended up bein' used in common English, provin' that gay folk have been educatin' the world since time began!

POPPERS

Nasty, stinky ole *amyl nitrate* is a legal drug, used mainly by gay guys ta git high.

Ah don't like it, but then Ah don't have ta sniff it!

POUFFE

In the UK this French originatin' word is a piece'a furniture that y'all put your feet up on, but it's also a hateful word ta mean gay guy, an' come's from a couple'a places, includin' rhymin' slang (see '**Nelly**') an' a 19th century word for an actor.

PRACTISING HOMOSEXUAL

If y'all do it enough y'all be real good at it! This means folk who like ta love the same sex, an' ain't ashamed'a it!

PRE/POST-OP

This is a guy who feels he's really a gal, or a gal who wants ta be a guy, an' are either waitin' ta git it changed, or have gone ahead an' done it.

PRETTY POLICEMAN

An officer'a the law who hangs out in cottages or tea rooms waitin' for gay guys ta git friendly with 'em, an' then arrests 'em for it. This is the kinda crap our hard earned taxes are bein' spent on an' it ticks me off!

PRIDE

This here annual celebration marks the anniversary'a The Stonewall Riots – with the first one bein' held in New York City on 28 June 1970, - an' now goes on in cities all over the world as a day for lbgt (an' straight!) folk ta git together, dress up an' party.

It used ta be way more political than it is nowadays, but is still a fun day out ta show folk that we're here, we're queer, an' we ain't goin' away!

PROVINCETOWN

A lil ole place in Cape Cod, Massachusetts, USA, this is one'a *the* vacation spots for gay guys an' gals! It came as a surprise ta me that it's also the original landin' site'a the Pilgrims, 'cause when the **Mayflower** got ta the USA in 1620 they stopped in Provincetown Harbour first'a all.

Ah'd say it's one'a the most wonderful places Ah've ever done visited, an' it sure did steal ma heart from San Francisco!

PROWLER

This store for gay guys an' (some!) gay gals first opened in London, England in 1997, an' provides all kinds'a goodies, from books ta bondage wear!

They now have stores all over the UK, an' are part'a the hugely successful gay company **Millivres.**

PUNK

Nowadays of course this means a kinda loud, fast, rock music first made famous in the 1970s, but the word itself comes from'a old term for a guy who went with other guys for money – said ta have been invented by **William Shakespeare** in the 16th century (the word, that is, not the thang itself!)

As an' innerestin' bit'a trivia folk reckon that the fashion for torn knees in ya jeans (made popular by the New York punk-rock band **The Ramones**) comes from the occupational hazard that workin' boys got from kneelin' down all'a the time!

PURE

Another term for a **Goldstar**

Q

QUEEN

Meanin' a camp gay guy, who folk reckon acts a lil bit girly an' regal.

Back in the 1970s singer **Freddy Mercury** (who surely knew somethin' about the subject!) formed the hugely popular rock band'a the same name in the UK.

QUEEN VICTORIA

This here Queen sure did us gay gals a favour, when in 1885 she (allegedly) announced ta all an' sundry that there weren't no way on earth that gals would do anythang sexual ta one an' other, 'cause it just weren't seemly!

So while it became illegal in the UK for gay guys ta git together, we gals never had ta fear the law when we got naked with each other (of course, gals didn't have no rights anyhow in them days, so it didn't really mean doodly-squat, but it's still kinda nice!)

QUEEN'S VERNACULAR

Provin' that some folk know a good idea when they see it, this lil ole book was writ by **Bruce Rodgers**, an' was the first published dictionary ta deal with slang used by, an' about, gay folk, an' it came out in San Francisco in 1972.

Ah swear on ma can'a Aqua Net that Ah ain't never seen nor read it, so don't git no funny ideas Mr Rodgers (just kiddin'!)

QUEER

Comin' from the German word **quer,** meanin' literally "not quite right", this got ta be used by the British as a mean ole term for gay folk in the 1920s, but'a course nowadays has been reclaimed, an' y'all can find heaps'a gay guys an' gals using it quite happily ta describe 'emselves.

QUEER NATION

Startin' out in 1990 in New York City, this bunch'a gay activists fight real hard ta git rights for gay folk, pullin' no punches along the way – they even done published a manifesto called "**Queers Read This**" (y'all can find it in the web address list at the back'a this here book) which sure is ta the point!

They're still goin' strong, an' they sure do raise a big ole ruckus, as well as a lot'a folk's consciousness.

QUIM

This here word has a couple'a meanin's, but it's mainly used for a gals down-stairs parts, an' some folk reckon it comes from the Welsh word **cwm**, meanin' 'valley' (Ah guess that kinda depends on what kinda life-style the gal in question has!) Other folk reckon it comes from an ole English word **queme,** which used ta mean somethin' kinda pleasurable, an' seems way nicer in ma opinion

Folk in the USA also use it as a kinda abusive term for the passive guy in a gay relationship. Back in the 1980s a bunch'a gay gals in the UK launched a raunchy ole magazine'a the same name, which was kinda the Brit gay gals version of "**On Our Backs**", an' had all kinds'a sexy stories an' pics ta titillate an' amuse.

QUORN-HORN

Some gay gals (ok, it's just me for now!) use this word ta mean a dildo, 'cause it ain't real meat, an' is way better for ya!

R

RADICAL FAERIES

Formed in San Francisco in 1979 by gay guys **Don Kilhefner**, **Mitch Walker** an' **Harry Hay** (who also started the **Mattachine Society**), these folk are Green an' rainbow at the same time! They're a spiritual, gentle bunch'a folk, who want'a lurve each other, an' the Earth itself, an' are all inclusive.

RED NECKTIE

Back in 1909 in Chicago, USA, the vice commission reckoned they could spot gay guys 'cause they wore red neckties as a sign ta tell each other they were gay!

This seemed ta catch on with gay guys, 'cause they carried on doin' this all through the 1940s an' 50s, but the trend kinda died down once gay rights came along an' folk didn't need ta be so subtle.

RED RIBBON

In 1991 New York artist **Frank Moore** got the idea'a creatin' a symbol for folk ta show their commitment ta helpin' fight AIDS an' HIV, an' ta generally show their support for folk who were livin' with the disease, so takin' his idea from all'a the yellow ribbons around at the time (ta support troops in the first Gulf War) he came up with this, which has now become known the world over as the sign'a AIDS charities.

RENT BOY

This here's a young guy who rents himself out for fun an' profit - well, mayhap it ain't that much fun for him, an' he probably don't make that much profit, but y'all git what Ah mean!

RIMMING

This is when folk like ta lick the outside'a their honey's ass.

ROCKY HORROR PICTURE SHOW, THE 🎬

Don't dream it, *be* it! This stage show an' movie paved the way for folk, both gay an' straight, ta dress up in basques, fish-nets and French-maids uniforms, an' ta forget about sexual oppression an' just have a darned good time.

It's still goin' strong today, with revivals all over the world, where folk go along dressed ta the nines, throw rice an' boogie, an' '*The Time-Warp*' has even become the unofficial theme song at *Kenric* discos!

ROOM-MATE

When folk don't want their family ta know they're livin' with a gay lover they try ta pass 'em off as this, but probably ain't foolin' no-one but their dumbest relative.

ROOSTER

This is here word from the 1920s means a tough acting butch dyke, who likes ta strut around the place – an' if y'all are real lucky she'll wake ya up at the crack'a dawn too!

ROSEANNE ☺

Roseanne is kinda my spiritual mom. Her TV sitcom, which ran from 1988 ta 1997, showed ordinary folk from the heartland of the USA goin' about their lives, but inna funny, sassy kinda way.

She pulled no punches, an' had plenty of gay folk on the show, from the uptight Leon (**Martin Mull**) ta wacky bisexual Nancy (**Sandra Bernhard**), with even Roseanne's mom (played by **Estelle Parsons**) comin' out as a gay gal! An' of course there's Darlene (**Sara Gilbert**), who wasn't a dyke on the show, but sure is in real life!

There was a big ole hoopla in 1994 when Roseanne had a smooch with another gal

(*Mariel Hemmingway*) in one episode, with ABC threatnin' not ta air it, (*Stephen Weisswasser*, an ABC spokesman, said '*the scene is not the lifestyle that most people lead.*') but when Roseanne threatened them right back an' said she'd go to another network they sure changed their minds about not showin' it!

She was also a successful stand-up, hosted her own chat-show (*The Roseanne Show*), an' even tried ta run for the Presidency of the USA in 2012!

Ah think she's' an all-round inspiration – but it sure is a shame that her singin' can make a grown gal cry!

ROUGH TRADE

This is a word from 1950s slang in the UK, an' it's a workin' class guy (who may or may not be gay) who goes with other guys, an' some gay guys find it kinda appealin' ta go with a guy who seems ta be kinda butch an' a lil bit scary

RUPAUL

Born in San Diego, CA, on 17 November 1960 *Rupaul Andre Charles* is a gorgeous drag queen, who now host his own TV (no pun intended!) show *Rupaul's Drag Race*.

He's also made some great dance music (ma favourite bein' **Supermodel**), been in bunch'a terrific movies (includin' the two fabulous the Brady Bunch "reboots, an' one'a ma favourites **But I'm a Cheerleader)**, an' writ hisself two books, *Lettin' It All Hang Out* an*' Workin' It!* *RuPaul's Guide to Life, Liberty, and the Pursuit of Style.*

S

S & M

Now known by a whole bunch'a other names
this means "sadism" an' "masochism"

Sadists are folk who like ta inflict pain durin' sex
(in a consensual way, of course) an' comes
from the **Marquis de Sade** (1740-1814), a
French guy who's innerest in pain got him sent
ta jail for 27 years, where he wrote a bunch'a
books, includin' '**120 Days of Sodom**' an' '**The
Crimes of Love**'

Masochists are the folk who like bein' hurt, an'
git their name from **Leopold von Sacher-
Masoch** (1836-1895), who writ the book
'**Venus in Furs**', about a guy named Severin
who sure did like ta be told off!

Neither one'a the guys (or their stories) are
actually gay, but gay folk have been enjoyin' (if
y'all can call it that!) S&M for many a year, an'
even have their own flag now (which is red,
black an' purple, an' really pretty ta ma mind!)

SAFE-SEX

This is when y'all take care'a yourselves an' each other, by makin' sure none'a them bodily fluid git inta places they ain't s'pose ta, an' is a level-headed response ta all kinds'a sexual infections, not just AIDS an' HIV.

SANDALS

Sandals offer "*a collection of 12 of the most romantic resorts on the Caribbean's best beaches*" accordin' ta their web-site, but up until 2004 this here paradise was only open ta straight folk, 'cause they catered ta couples only, an' believed that a couple was "*one female adult and one male adult*", an' that "*couples of the same gender aren't accepted*", a policy which caused gay folk ta kick up the dickens, an' git some'a their adverts banned, which Ah'm sure went a long way ta gittin' the company ta change their minds.

SAN FRANCISCO

Gayest city in the world (especially Castro Street). Seems ta be the cradle of most gay thangs!

SANTA CLAUS

An older gay guy who likes ta treat his chicken ta gifts, an' Ah guess there might be some candy cane lickin' involved too…

SAPPHIC

Follower'a **Sappho** – though not 'cause we all write poems!

SAPPHO

Born in 630 BC on the Greek island Lesvos, this poet ran a school for gals, where it's said she taught 'em ta write their own ditties, an' plenty more besides!

There ain't much'a her poetry around no more, mainly 'cause her reputation as a gal-lurvin' gal riled up the Christian church, but her influence was so strong that **William Shakespeare** referred ta her as "*the 10th muse*", an'a course the name'a her birth-place is the reason we gay gals are called lesbians.

SCENE, THE

What gay folk call the places they'all go ta meet each other an' party, which can'a course be bars, clubs, cruisin' areas or any other such social place.

SCENERY

A mighty fine lookin' straight person, who y'all can't have, but who y'all can look at an' admire

SCIENTOLOGY ☹

Proof that it ain't just Christians who hate us, this here club for crackpots with way too much money was started in 1953 by *L. Ron Hubbard*, an' aside from a whole bunch'a weird-assed beliefs they'all think that *"the sexual pervert (and by this term...includes any and all forms of deviation...such as homosexuality, lesbianism, sexual sadism, etc...is actually quite ill physically."* an' that we'all should:
"Be taken from the society as rapidly as possible and uniformly institutionalized; for here is the level of the contagion of immorality, and the destruction of ethics...no social order will survive which does not remove these people from its midst." (Quotes taken from *"Dianetics: The Modern Science of Mental Health"*)

Ah guess if this means never havin' ta watch a shitty **Tom Cruise** movie again it can only be a good thang, but that's 'cause they'all make me mad enough ta split!

SCISSORING

Ah personally cain't figure out how this here act works, 'cause it does sound like'a lotta effort (but Ah'm open ta bein' educated!). It's when two gay gals get pussy ta pussy, an' is called this causa'a how it looks. It's also how the real gay friendly pop band **The Scissor Sisters** got their name.

SECTION 28

Well now, how do Ah begin ta describe this here lil ole nugget'a bull-spit?

Back in the 1980s the UK was run by the **Conservative Party**, - with **Margaret Thatcher** as dictator... Ah'm sorry, Ah mean Prime Minister! - , a bunch'a folk not exactly famous for bein' enlightened an' liberal. They'all got kinda worked up by gay folk havin' rights an' such, an' on 24 May 1988 brought out this law which said that local government weren't allowed ta:

"intentionally promote homosexuality or publish material with the intention of promoting homosexuality" or *"promote the*

teaching in any maintained school of the acceptability of homosexuality as a pretended family relationship",

which was so fuzzy that it could'a applied ta any an' every thang!

Folk got real mad, an' there were protests an' demonstrations up an' down the country, includin' some real funny an' inventive stuff (see '**A**' an' '**B**' for some'a the best ones!), but it weren't until the UK got a Labour government that this evil law got repealed on 18 November 2003.

Sh! WOMEN'S EROTIC EMPORIUM

Ah always kid that goin' ta gay pride used'a be about fightin' ta end oppression, but nowadays it's about fightin' ta git inta the Sh! tent – an' if any'a y'all have ever seen it y'all know why!

Startin' out on 1 April 1992 in London, UK, this lil store is the British equivalent'a *Good Vibrations,* an' is run by gals *for* gals'a all persuasions, who want'a git in on good style!

SIGNIFICANT OTHER

Classy folk use this ta describe their honey-bun or main squeeze.

SIMPSONS, THE

These lil yeller folk created by **Matt Groening** in 1989 sure are funny, but they also cover a bunch'a issues, includin' heaps'a stuff about gay folk.

'**Homersphobia**' had a guest spot from movie director **John Waters**, who as a gay guy freaked Homer out at first, when he thought Bart might 'catch' gay off'a him, an' in '**There's Something About Marrying**' their hometown Springfield legalised gay marriage, which got Homer cashin' in, an' had Marge's sister Patty comin' out as a gay gal! An'a course, they got Smithers, who seems kinda gay ta me!

The show might'a also given someone an idea for a name, but Ah ain't sayin' no more about that!

SISTERS OF PERPETUAL INDULGANCE

Lordy be, the hills sure are alive when these sisters are out an' about!

Startin' out by borrowin' habits from a bunch'a Roman Catholic nuns in Iowa, USA (ta perform '**The Sound of Music**' of course!) in 1976, these 'gals' then took ta the streets'a San Francisco in 1979 ta raise a hoopla at Easter weekend, an' have been makin' appearances ever since!

They now have 'orders' all over the States, an' also in Australia, Europe, an' even Uruguay, an' can be guaranteed ta bring smiles ta the faces'a folk at many gay events!

SIZE QUEEN

Gay guy who wants more than average from his lovers, if y'all git what Ah mean!

SOAPS (in the UK)

Ah do sure lurve ma stories, an' they've proven ta be a hotbed'a ground breakin' stuff showing LGBT tales.

In the UK **Brookside** was the first ta ever show ta have gay an' lesbian characters (Gordon Collins played by **Nigel Cowley** an' then **Mark Burgess**) an' Beth Jordache (played by **Anna Friel**) – who also got ta have the first lesbian kiss in a UK soap.

Not ta be outdone **EastEnders** have had a whole mess'a firsts – first gay kiss between two guys when characters Guido Smith (**Nicholas Donovan**) an' Colin Russell (**Michael Cashman**) smooched it up, promptin' dumbass viewers ta go inta a meltdown'a complainin'.

EastEnders has also notched up the first ever interracial kiss between two day gals (although Ah might be wrong but Ah think all'a their gay gal couples have been that way!), the first gay weddin', an' the first ever lesbian adoption story.

An' the longest runnin' UK soap, *Coronation Street* made big ole steps when they innerduced the first ever trans character in a British soap, in the form'a Hayley Patterson played by *Julie Hesmondhalgh*.

Ah know folk in the rest'a the world watch their own stories, an' that they got a heap'a LGBT characters too, but that would fill a whole library'a books!

SODOMY

This here now pretty much mean's takin' it up the butt, an' comes from that tired ole Bible story (Genesis, Chapter 19) about Lot, his wife, an' their daughters.

SOLANAS, VALERIE

Born on 9 April 1936, in New Jersey, USA, this bi-gal had a pretty awful childhood, which left her kinda cracked, an' when she wasn't tryin' ta off *Andy Warhol* (which she tried – an' failed – ta do on 3 June 1968) , could be found either turnin' tricks or pennin' her infamous book "*The*

S.C.U.M Manifesto", which advocates killin' guys (S.C.U.M standin' for the 'society for cutting up men'), a cheery lil tome, which is kinda crude, but could be said ta be a forerunner ta the women's liberation movement.

Ole Val died on 26 April 1988 in San Francisco, an' a pretty good movie called '*I Shot Andy Warhol*' – starrin' *Lili Taylor* as Val an' *Jared Harris* as Andy - came out about her in 1996.

SPARE RIB

This was a British feminist magazine that got started in June 1972.

'Cause it dealt with all kinds'a issues for gals, both gay an' straight, many stores wouldn't carry the title, but despite that foolishness the magazine carried on for another 21 years, an' helped out many a gal who wanted ta live her own life an' not be told what ta do by guys.

SPARTACUS

When this movie, directed by *Stanley Kubrick*, an' starrin' *Kirk Douglas* in the title role, first came out in 1960 it had a big ole scene missin', 'cause it dealt with gay stuff, but was finally put back together in 1991.

In the scene *Laurence Olivier's* character Crassus is tryin' ta figure out if his slave Antoninus (played by *Tony Curtis*) is inta guys or gals, by askin' him if he likes ta eat oysters or snails, an' if one is morally better than the other – ta which Antoninus replies that its all the same ta him, or some-such thang.

Ta ma mind that whole conversation is kind'a a head-scratcher, mayhap 'cause Ah don't like ta eat either of 'em, an' don't believe Crassus would'a given a rats-ass what his slave preferred, he would'a just done it anyway! Still, it's good ta see the movie back in its uncensored form.

SPARTACUS INTERNATIONAL GAY GUIDE

Since 1970 this here guide has been tellin' gay guys where ta go in the best possible way!

It covers everythang from where ta go for the best bars, clubs an' hotels, ta warnin' folk about any scary ole laws that may exist in the vacation spot they want ta visit

148

SPRINGFIELD, DUSTY ☺

Born **Mary O'Brien** on 16 April 1939 in London, England, dusty was a big ole singin' star in the 1960s, who had a bunch'a fantastic hit records, includin' '**I Only Want To Be With You**', '**Son Of A Preacher Man**' an' ma personal favourite song about gittin' it on, '**The Look Of Love**', most'a which were penned by **Burt Bacharach**.

She was also an outspoken gal, refusin' ta perform ta white-only audiences in the then segregated South Africa in 1964, which led ta her gittin' kicked out'a the country, an' tellin' the British newspaper **The Evening Standard** in 1970 that she liked gals as well as guys

After havin' a few problems in the 70s due ta booze an' coke she made a big ole come-back in the late 1980s, thanks ta pop group **The Pet Shop Boys**, with records such as "**What Have I Done To Deserve This?**" an' "**In Private**".

Sadly, Dusty passed on 2 March 1999 from breast cancer, an' Ah for one believe the world lost a great star. R.I.P Dusty

STONE BUTCH

A gay gal who likes ta give but don't like ta receive anythang in return (an' Ah ain't talkin' birthday presents here!)

STONEWALL (INN AND RIOT)

On 28 June 1969 gay folk at **The Stonewall Inn** in New York City finally got sick'a bein' hassled by the cops, an' began resistin' arrest an' throwin' bricks at 'em, leadin' ta a big ole riot that lasted until the next day, an' the birth'a the gay rights movement.

Some folk reckon the whole thang took place 'cause some'a the gay guys were in mournin' for **Judy Garland**, who'd died six days previously, but Ah reckon they'd just had enough, an' say good for them!

STONEWALL (MOVIE) 🎬

Made in 1995 by director **Nigel Finch**, this lil gem of a movie tells the story'a the harassment the gay guys had ta put up with, an' the riot that came after.

It's got a cool soundtrack by *The Shangri-La's* an' such, an' is on ma list'a recommended viewin'!

STONEWALL ORGANISATION

Startin' in London, England in 1989, an' takin' its name from the famous bar in New York, this group began by protestin' Section 28, an' have since been workin' ta help end the oppression of gay folk, includin' campaignin' ta git the age'a consent lowered for gay guys, so'as it became equal with straight folk, gittin' gay folk the right ta wed, an' all manner'a thangs ta make our lives better.

STRAIGHT-ACTING

This is a gay guy or gal who don't really want folk ta know what they are, so try real hard ta hide it.

STUD

Bless 'em, those young 'uns keep comin' up with new words ta call themselves, an' this is a new word for "butch" that's sweepin' the States!

SWISH

Originally comin' from the rustlin' noise made by a gal's dress back in the 1800s, this then got ta mean a girly way'a walkin', an' in the 1930s became a word for a camp gay guy.

SWITCH-HITTER

Another term for those folk who like ta go both ways when it comes ta love – an' in comes from electricity switchin' from AC to DC.

SYLVESTER ☺

Born on 6 September 1948, in Los Angeles, USA, this guy ruled the gay disco scene in the 1970s an' 80s, with great dance songs like '*You Make Me Feel (Mighty Real)*' an' '*Do You Wanna Funk?*'

He was an' out an' out camp gay guy, who refused ta act butch', an' took ta dressin' in drag ta tick folk off!

He sadly passed on 16 December 1988, as a result'a AIDS, but can still git those asses shakin' on the dance floor in clubs the world over today.

T

TEAROOM

This is what gay guys in the USA call a public bathroom used as a meetin' place for all kinds'a exchanges. Some folk reckon it comes from slang for **t**oilet room

TEENA, BRANDON

This is one'a the saddest entries in this book. Born **Teena Brandon** in Lincoln, Nebraska, on 12 December 1972, this non-op trans-man had ta deal with shit from the word go, includin' bein' abused an' neglected, an' havin' a generally god-awful childhood.

In 1993 he moved ta Richardson County, Nebraska, where he took up with a local gal **Lana Tisdel**, an' got ta know the two prime assholes who would end up killin' him, **Marvin Nissen** an' **John L Lotter**.

Bein' the ignorant, nasty sons a' bitches they were these two guys couldn't get their heads 'round Brandon bein' the way he was, an' raped him. Then on 31 December 1993 they broke inta the house he was in with Lana an' shot Brandon, then finished off the job'a killin' him by stabbing him ta death.

In 1999 a movie was made'a his sadly short life, **Boys Don't Cry**, written by **Kimberly Peirce** an' **Andy Bienen**, an' starrin' **Hilary Swank** as Brandon, which helped bring his sufferin' ta light, and ta hopefully educate people ta the mindless, vicious crap that LGBT folk suffer every day at the hands'a idiot scumbags.

THERON, CHARLIZE

This gal ain't gay, but she sure is cool! Apart from bein' a fantastic actress (see her Oscar winnin' role as **Aileen Wuornos** in the 2003 movie **Monster** for proof'a that!) Charlize has stated that she won't wed until us gay folk can legally do the same in the USA! Way ta go gal!

THIRD SEX

Karl Heinrich Ulrichs came up with this here term for gay folk in the 1800s, with the first sex bein' a straight guy, an' the second being a straight gal

TOM/TOMBOY

Back in the middle'a the 1500s this used ta mean a workin' gal (comin' from the French word **tomber** – meanin' ta 'take a tumble') but cause them gals weren't considered lady-like it got changed by the end'a that century ta mean a gal who acted all kinda boisterous an' a lil bit masculine.

Even so, some folk in the UK still use tom in its original way.

TOM OF FINLAND

Touko Laaksonen, born 8 May 1920, in Kaarina, Finland, sure did like his guys big an' beefy, and drew a whole mess'a pictures'a huge, uniformed guys doin' all manner'a thangs ta one another! Boy-howdy, some'a them fellahs have got equipment that'll make ya eyes water just lookin' at it!

TOP

A guy or gal who likes ta do all the work between the sheets, or anywhere else for that matter!

TOP SURGERY

When a gal has her titties taken away as part'a her gender re-assignment surgery ta become a guy.

TORCH SONG TRILOGY 🎬

This here's one'a ma favourite movies, which came out in 1988, though it was originally a New York stage production in 1978.

It tells the story'a Arnold Beckoff, a torch singer an' drag queen, an' his struggle for love an' acceptance, an' even though it gets kinda sad, by the end everythang comes out right an' it's a real upliftin' story. Arnold was played by **Harvey Fierstein** in both the stage an' screen versions, an' he also writ the thang itself. Go check it out, y'all be glad ya did!

TRADE

Yet another word for a guy for hire – an' Ah don't mean no handy man, though that kinda fits the definition too!

TRANSGENDER/TRANSEXUAL

This is a guy or gal who ain't happy that way, an' who takes steps ta rectify the situation, by either dressin' an' living as the opposite sex, or by goin' ahead an' havin' surgery ta really feel the part, (see the meanin'a *tran* below)

TRANS-MAN

A guy who used ta be a gal.

TRANSPHOBIC

Some folk just don't like anythang that's a lil bit different, and this here term means folk who can't stand the idea of the guys an' gals mentioned above (phobic literally meanin' 'fear' in Greek). Ah say anyone who's got the guts an' determination ta change somethin' that they feel is wrong, an' don't hurt no-one else in the process should be celebrated an' not feared, so git real folk!

TRANSVESTITE

A guy (not always gay) who likes ta wear dresses, panty-hose an' all the kinda stuff that gals are usually s'posed ta wear, an' was invented by German guy **Magnus Hirschfeld** in 1910, from the Latin words "**trans**", meanin' "**the opposite**" an' "**vestere**", meanin' "**ta dress**"

Innerestingly enough, this don't seem ta apply ta gals who like ta wear pants an' other 'traditional' guy clothes, which is kinda prejudiced ta ma mind!

TRIBADISM

This is when two gay gals git inta position an' rub their pussies together (don't git jumpy, y'all know Ah ain't talkin' about felines here!), an' it comes from the Greek word *tribein*, meanin' ta rub.

TRICK

Originally meanin' the customer'a a workin' guy or gal, this started ta mean a gay guy's lil bit'a fun at the beginnin'a the 1900s – an' it comes from the Latin word *tricae*, which means somethin' that ain't all that serious.

TROLL

This is a kinda mean word that gay guys use for unattractive guys who hang out in cruisin' areas, an' who git kinda persistent when tryin' ta git attention, an' it comes from them ugly critters that hang out under bridges an' bug folk in fairy stories.

TROLLING

When a gay guy goes out lookin' for lurve in the great outdoors, an' just don't quit until he gets some.

TURKEY BASTER

If a couple'a gay gals have gotta kid y'all might wanna think twice about eatin' Thanksgivin' or Christmas dinner at their place 'cause this ole thang is now kinda linked ta artificial insemination!

TWILIGHT WORLD

Back in the 1950s bein' gay was illegal, an' had ta be a big ole secret – so gay folk kinda lived in the 'ordinary' world most'a the time, an' in this one when they wanted ta be 'emselves.

TWIN PEAKS TAVERN

This lil ole bar on Castro Street in San Francisco is kinda important, cause back when it opened in 1972 bein' openly gay was still kinda taboo, but **Peggy Forster** an' **Mary Ellen Cunha**, the two gay gals who ran the place decided it should be the first gay bar in the USA ta have big ole clear glass windows ta show the world there ain't nothin' secret or nasty about gay folk.

TWINK

This is a 1980s term for a cute gay guy, an' it takes its name from the lil ole sponge cake the **Twinkie**, made by the **Continental Baking Company**, which is yummy an' full'a white stuff that some folk love ta eat – y'all just better check whether or not it's good for ya before y'all chow down, if y'all git what Ah mean!

TWINKIE DEFENCE

When **Dan White** shot **Harvey Milk** (see '**M**' for more information) part'a his defence for doin' it was cause he was all pumped up on sugar from eatin' too many'a the cakes mentioned above, an' drinkin' too much **Coca Cola**, which folk rightly took ta be bull-spit. After all, eatin' too much sugar might turn y'all inta a lard-ass, but it don't often turn y'all inta a (murdering) dumb-ass!

U

UGLY BETTY

Betty weren't gay (she weren't ugly for that matter, either), but the show sure represented folk from the lavender life in a pretty positive way!

There was ornery yet sometimes kinda sweet Marc St. James, Betty's nephew Justin (played by two out an' proud gay guys *Michael Urie* an' *Mark Indelicato* respectively) and trans-gal Alexis Meade (*Rebecca Romijn*) The show ran from September 2006 ta April 2010, an' was proof that things were slowly changin' for the better in TV Land.

UKIP

United Kingdom Independence Party – these folk pay lip service ta bein' concerned an' reasoned, but like all assholes sometimes the doo-doo leaks out!

UKIP member *Iain McLaughlan* is all for bringin' back Section 28, while *Douglas Denny* said that gay folk are 'abnormal', an' gay guys in particular are 'disgusting'.

However the dumbest of 'em all (so far - this bunch has more dummies than Mothercare!) was **David Silvester**, who done said that the awful floods in the UK in 2013/14 were due ta the Conservatives allowin' gay folk ta wed:

"*The scriptures make it abundantly clear that a Christian nation that abandons its faith and acts contrary to the Gospel (and in naked breach of a coronation oath) will be beset by natural disasters such as storms, disease, pestilence and war.*"

These guys can be seen as fools, but Ah get an uneasy feelin' about 'em, especially now that folk seem ta be votin' for their "let's blame all our problems on *the others*" BS.

KARL-HEINRICH ULRICHS

Born on 28 August 1825, in Aurich, Germany, this guy did more ta help spread intelligent information about gay folk than anyone else at the time.

In 1862 he began writin' under the pen-name **Numa Numantius**, tellin' everyone he was gay, an' that there weren't a darn thang wrong with bein' that way!

'Course, he got inta a bunch'a trouble with the law for bein' so open, an' his writin's got banned in 1864, but he kept right on at it, publishing twelve books all together before his death on 14 July 1895. In the course'a all this writin' he came up with a bunch'a new words for gay folk, which are shown below.

UNCLOSETED

Gay folk who have seen the light outside'a that ole closet door, an' tell the world that they're gay, an' that it ain't nothin' ta be ashamed about.

UNNATURAL

Paul of Tarsus is said ta have writ a big ole part'a the new testament'a **The Bible,** an' he sure did have a problem with gay folk!

Part'a his leavin's is ta have innerduced the idea that gay folk are against nature, when he described us as this (usin' the Greek phrase for it **para physin)** in Romans 1:26-27 – which has'a course led ta all those twisted Christian folk hatin' us ever since – even though there's now a whole bunch'a proof that bein' gay ain't just a human thang, but goes on in every kinda life-form.

URANIAN/URANIANISM

This is a term for a gay guy that was thought up by **Karl-Heinrich Ulrichs** (see above) in 1864, an' he got the idea from the Greek word

Uranos, which in turn is s'posed ta come from the philosopher *Plato*, who reckoned that the god *Uranus* was the first guy ta be gay! (an' Ah don't wanna hear no snickerin' from y'all!)

URANO-DIONING:

Ah've explained all about Uranian stuff above, but ole Karl also used the term *Dioning* (from the Greek Titan goddess *Dione*) for a guy who likes gals, so this here term was his way'a referrin' to a bi-guy.

URNING

A guy who's kinda fond of Uranian practices (see above).

V

V.G.F

Some folk who don't like ta let on that their honey *is* their honey git kinda antsy an' refer ta 'em as their "**v**ery **g**ood **f**riend"

VANGUARD

Back in 1966 in San Francisco, USA, a bunch'a gay guys workin' the streets got together an' formed this, the first ever organization'a its kind, ta git better protection for 'emselves, an' ta generally help other young gay folk in the city

VANILLA

Folk who like their sexual doin's ta be kinda plain and ordinary. Nothin' wrong with that!

VERSATILE

This here is a guy or gal who likes ta turn their hands (an' many other body parts!) ta all kinds'a thangs in the bedroom

VETERANS BENEVOLENT ASSOCIATION

Started in 1945 in New York City, this was one'a the earliest gay groups in the USA, an' was for gay folk who got kicked outta the military. It was kinda a place for folk ta meet an' get ta know each other, but they had a big ole bust up about what they were doin', an' parted ways in 1954

VICE-VERSA

Way back in June 1947 in Los Angeles, USA, a gay gal callin' herself **Lisa Ben** (git a pen an' paper an' go figure that out for yaselves!) bought this out, which was the first ever mag for gay gals, an' known at the time as "America's gayest magazine".

Lisa was actually called **Edith Eyde**, an' sadly she only produced nine editions'a the mag, an' even then only got out ten copies'a each edition, but any gal that managed ta git a copy must'a sure been glad that she did!

VICTIM

This here movie, directed by **Basil Dearden**, an' starrin' **Dirk Bogarde** an' **Sylvia Syms**, came out in 1961, an' was the first British movie ever ta deal with gay guys in a more positive way, an' the first time the word "homosexual" was ever used in a movie.

It's the story'a Melville Farr, a married barrister who fights ta bring a bunch'a guys who blackmail gay guys (bein' gay was still illegal in the UK at the time) ta justice, despite knowin' that he'll have ta come outta the closet himself ta do it.

Folk reckon that this movie helped ta influence the guys who were workin' on the **Wolfenden Report** (see '**W**') at the time, which in turn led ta gay guys – over 21, 'a course - finally bein' allowed ta legally lurve each other in the uk.

W

WALKER

This is a young gay guy who squires a straight gal in her golden years around town, but he ain't acting as her beard, he's just bein' a good guy an' keepin' her company.

WATCH QUEEN

When y'all are doin' the do inna cottage or tea room this is the guy who gets ta keep an eye out for any pryin' law-men

WATERS, JOHN ☺

Well, strap me down an' fill me full'a liquid eye-liner! If **Roseanne** is ma spiritual mom then this fabulous gay guy sure is ma spiritual pop!

Born on 22 April 1946, in Baltimore, USA, John is responsible for some'a the sickest – an' funniest – movies ever made!

Startin' in 1964 with '**Hag In A Black Leather Jacket**', an' with his most recent movie (at the time'a writin') bein' '**A Dirty Shame**', released in 2004, he's written an' directed 16 movies, all dealin' with the kinda stuff that folk don't talk about in polite comp'ny.

His most infamous movie has ta be '**Pink Flamingos**', an' made a big ole star outta **Glenn Harris Milstead** aka **Divine**, with the last scene prob'ly bein' one'a the grossest thangs ever committed ta celluloid – if y'all have seen it y'all know what Ah mean, an' if ya ain't don't eat a candy bar while ya watch it!

He kinda got more respectable when the movie '**Hairspray**' came out in 1988, though he still brings out stuff that's beautifully twisted an' is a real antidote ta brain-rottin' Hollywood blockbusters. Here's ta the next one – though Ah wish he'd get a damn move on! -

Though folk, Ah have ta say Ah ain't happy about the 2007 remake'a '**Hairspray**' by director **Adam Shankman** - Ah don't care if John's in it, an' disagrees with ma thinkin' in his book "**Role Models**", but ta ma mind any movie starrin' a Scientologist in one'a Divine's role's is just plain wrong!

WEEBLE

Harsh ole term for a **troll**, 'cause they usually hang around but never go down. Named after a toy for young 'uns.

WELL OF LONELINESS

This depressin' ole book about a gal who loves gals, but sure ain't too gay about it, was writ by **Radclyffe Hall** in 1928 (see '**H**' for way more information) Don't expect ta have ya ribs (or anythang else!) tickled when y'all read it folk!

WEST, KANYE

This successful rap an' hip-hop singer ain't a gay guy hisself, but is real cool anyhow, even though he has a knack'a pissin' folk off a lotta the time!

Back in 2005 he told MTV that "*hip hop is about speaking your mind and about breaking down barriers, but everyone in hip-hop discriminates against gay people*" an' I *wanna just, to come on TV and just tell my rappers, just tell my friends, 'yo, stop it'*, an' he stands by that even though a lotta dumb folk gave him a ton'a shit for sayin' it.

WESTENHOEFER, SUZANNE ☺

Born on 31 March 1961, in Pennsylvania, USA, Suzanne has got ta be one'a the funniest gay gals around!

Since the early 1990s she's been makin' folk pee their pants with laughter across the USA, an' beyond, an' has released three fantastic cds an' dvds'a her stand-up routines, which are a must have for any gay gal's trailer!

WHAT DO LESBIANS DO IN BED?

Ah had ta add this 'cause folk (includin' gay guys, shame on y'all!) still ask this dumb ole question! So gals, if anyone asks, just sing 'em this here song Ah made up special for y'all (y'all should know the tune from **Annie Get Your Gun!**):

'Anythang y'all can do,
We can do for longer,
We can do everythang,
An' we can do it all night!'

WHEEL-CHAIR SET

Ah'll be hog tied – gay folk sure have a knack'a findin' mean words for each other. Some gay guys use this ta mean other guys who are kinda past their prime. Boys, we all get a lil grey 'round the gusset eventually!

WHITE NIGHT RIOTS

When, on 21 May 1979, ole Twinkie-breath **Dan White** got a piddly lil prison term for killin' **Harvey Milk** (see '**M**') a whole bunch'a angry gay folk started ta gather on Castro Street in San Francisco, USA.

They moved down from the Castro ta City Hall, growin' in number until there were thousands'a folk, where they began ta smash the place up, an' generally vent their fury on any piece'a property in sight – includin' a bunch'a cop cars. Later on that night the San Francisco police department retaliated by comin' down ta the Castro an' beatin' up on gay folk an' smashin' up *The Elephant Walk* bar, which got the gay folk all riled up again, turnin' inta a big ole riot, an' an important landmark for gay folk fighting injustice everywhere.

WHITEHOUSE, MARY

Ole Mary, born 13 June 1910, had way too much time on her hands, an' spent most'a her life bitchin' an' moanin' about stuff that she considered 'immoral'.

As well as any kinda sexual references on TV or in print she got her panties in a wad over blasphemy, 'cause she was a good ole god-fearin' gal, an' in 1976 she privately prosecuted the British mag *Gay News* for printin'a a poem called '*The Love That Dare Not Speak Its Name*' by *James Kirkup*, cause it was about a Roman centurion who fantasized about havin' sex with the body'a Jesus when he got took down from the cross (which Ah've read, an' have ta say, even Ah find it kinda wrong, sorry folk – but Ah wouldn't stop other folk from readin' it!)

She won the case, an' *Gay News Ltd* an' editor *Denis Lemon* got fined £1500 between 'em, with Denis gittin' a suspended jail sentence'a nine months, thought this was over-turned in 1978

Mary was a big ole buddie'a **Margaret Thatcher**, an' in 1980 she got given a *CBE* for her services ta small-mindedness, or some such thang, but went home ta her lord on 23 November 2001, where Ah bet she's been spinnin' with horror at what goes on nowadays ever since!

WILDE, OSCAR ☺

Born on 16 October 1854, in Dublin, Ireland, Oscar sure was a witty guy, an' led a real innerestin' life, that's for sure!

He's best known for writin' a bunch'a plays, poems an' stories, includin' *'The Importance Of Being Earnest'* an' *'The Picture Of Dorian Gray'*, but is also kinda well known as bein' a gay guy too!

He got involved with a guy called **Lord Alfred Douglas**, who he called '**Bosie**', an' when this fellah's pop (*The Marquess of Queensberry*) writ Oscar a note callin' him gay, Oscar (kinda dumbly, if y'all ask me) took him ta court for libel on 3 April 1895.

Durin' the trail it'a course came out that Oscar *was* gay, an' he ended up gittin' arrested, an' on 25 May 1895 he got sentenced ta 2 years hard labour in jail. He got released on 19 May 1897, but prison had made him real sick, an' he eventually died on 30 November 1900.

WILL AND GRACE

This sitcom, about a gay guy an' his straight gal buddy, ran from September 1998 ta May 2006, It starred **Eric McCormack** as Will Truman, an' **Debra Messing** as Grace, but ta ma mind should'a been called Jack (**Sean Hayes)** an' Karen (**Megan Mullally**) 'cause they were way funnier!

WIMBLEDON

Now Ah know that there's a whole bunch'a other tennis tournaments the world over, but dagnabit, Ah'm only writin' about the ones in the UK!

First startin' in 1877, an' held every year since then durin' June an' July this lil ole championship has seen some'a the greatest gay gals ta hit the court.

There's been **Billie Jean King, Martina Navratilova, Conchita Martinez,** an' **Amélie Mauresmo**, an' Ah'm sure there'll be a whole bunch more in years ta come, 'cause gay gals seem ta do really well at the sport (straight gals do too'a course, but this book ain't about them!)

WIMMIN/WOMYN

Back in the 1970s feminists an' gay gals didn't want folk ta consider 'em as havin' anythang ta do with guys, so they took ta spellin' the word 'woman' in all kinds'a new ways so'as ta leave out the 'man' part.

WOLFENDEN REPORT

Back in the early 1950s gay guys in the UK could git sent ta jail for life if they were caught with another guy, an' this seemed pretty dumb ta some enlightened folk at the time!

On 15 September 1954 14 guys an' gals (includin' chairman **Lord John Wolfenden**) got together ta look inta this sorry state'a affairs, an' over the course'a 62 days innerviewed a bunch'a folk ta try an' sort thangs out.

At the end'a their debatin' they decided that "*homosexual behaviour between consenting adults in private should no longer be a criminal offence*", an' set about tryin' ta change it, but it weren't until 27 July 1967 that gay guys over the age'a 21 were finally allowed ta lurve one an' other in the eyes'a the law.

WOMANIST

This here word was coined by writer **Alice Walker**, in her 1983 book '**In Search Of Our Mothers' Gardens: Womanist Prose**', an' she originally used it ta describe the struggle for feminist independence for black gals, but other gals have since taken it on ta mean a gal of any colour who loves an' respects other gals.

X

XENA THE WARRIOR PRINCESS

Ah reckon this lil ole TV show is gonna give some good ole memories ta gay gals for years ta come!

First hittin' the small screen in 1995, an' runnin' for 6 seasons until its end in 2001, the show featured the adventures of butt-kickin' tough gal Xena (played by New Zealander *Lucy Lawless*) an' her best buddy Gabrielle (played by Texan gal *Renée O'Connor*), as they fought all kinds'a bad guys an' critters in ancient Greece.

Xena an' Gabrielle may'a had various guy beaux durin' their time together, but that didn't stop 'em gittin' all up-close an' personal with each other from time ta time – an' Xena even managed ta git knocked up by a gal (evil ole Callisto, played by *Hudson Leick*), an' ta ma mind there ain't been a show ta compare since!

X CHROMOSOME

Back in 1994 **Dean Hamer** figured out that some mom's kept havin' gay sons, an' when he looked inta it discovered that this could be down ta the mom's bodies somehow makin' the x chromosomes that they passed on inactive.

Since then a whole bunch'a other folk have looked inta it, an' have pretty much come ta the same conclusion an' have named the part that does this the *xq28*

X QUEEN

This is a young gay guy who likes ta party, an' is kinda partial ta takin' the drug Ecstasy (aka **MDMA**). Ah guess that's all well an' good, but will he still lurve ya tomorrow?

XXL

Started in 2000 in London by **Mark Ames**, an' still goin' strong, this is *the* British club for bears and the folk who like 'em – so if y'all want a big ole Yogi ta check out ya basket y'all know where ta go!

Y

YAOI

This here is an acronym **yama nashi, ochi nashi, imi nashi**, an' it translates ta "no climax, no point, no meaning", an' is a form'a Japanese Manga showin' gay guys lurvin' each other

YEOMANETTE

This is a 1960s term for a young gay guy in the US Navy – though how folk would'a known is a mystery ta me, seein' as it weren't legal in them days! Ah guess they had ta know each other pretty well!

YESTERGAY

First bein' used in the 1990s, this refers ta folk who used ta be gay, but ain't no more

YMCA

This lil ole tune about the **Young Men's Christian Association** was a chart hit for **The Village People** in 1979, an' while nowadays y'all might find ya granmaw dancin' an' spellin' out the letters at a weddin' reception, when it first came out it caused more fuss than a possum in a tub'a molasses, 'cause many folk thought it was all about gay guys goin' down ta the place an' hookin' up with other guys!

<u>YOUNG, WILL</u>

Born on 20 January 1979, in Berkshire, UK, Will was the first ever winner'a ITV's music contest **Pop Idol** in 2002, an' as soon as he won it he came out an' told the world he was a gay guy, which is a pretty cool thang ta do.

Ole Will went on ta great success, an' has had over a dozen hit records in the UK an' beyond at the time'a writin'.

<u>YOYO</u>

A late 1990s term for a guy who can't decide if he likes the gals or the guys more, an' swings back an' forth between the two.

<u>YURI</u>

Literally meanin' "lily" in Japanese this is the name for gay gals in Manga comics

Z

ZAMI

This here's a Caribbean word, from the isle'a Carriacou, an' it means a bunch'a black gals livin' an' lurvin' together, an' was first popularised by writin' gal **Audre Lorde** (see '**L**') in her 1982 book '**Zami: A New Spelling of My Name**'

ZANIE

Comin' ta mean a gay guy in the middle'a the 19th century, this used'a ta mean a bunch'a crazy actin' an' colourful clowns from Italy back in the 15th century. It's kinda fallen outta favour now, 'cause there ain't too many gay guys who wanta be considered clown-like.

ZAP

One'a them cuttin' yet witty insults that gay guys seem ta be so good at.

ZIPPER

In 1983 Millivres Ltd open the first gay store for guys ta buy all kinds'a goodies, from magazines ta the kinda toys that y'all need ta be all growed up for. Over the years it turned inta **Prowler**, an' is still goin' strong with that name today.

ZIPPER CLUB

Not ta be confused with a supper club, this here's a back room in a bar or club where Ah'm guessin' y'all can still get a tasty treat ta fill ya mouth.

HANKY CODES

Ah dunno if many gay guys still use these here
codes, but just in case y'all
were wonderin'...:

Left pocket	Colour	Right pocket
Chubby	Apricot	Chubby Chaser
Rimmee	Beige	Rimmer
Heavy S&M Top	Black	Heavy S&M Bottom
Scat Top	Brown	Scat Bottom
Uncircumcised	Brown Lace	Likes uncircumcised dicks
Circumcised	Brown Satin	Likes circumcised dicks
Biker	Chamois	Likes Bikers

Latex Top	Charcoal	Latex Bottom
Suck Ma Toes	Coral	Toe-sucker
Tit Torturer	Dark Pink	Tit Torturee
Double Fister	Dark Red	Double Fistee
Cottage Top	Doily	Cottage Bottom
Spanker	Fuscia	Spankee
2 Looking for 1	Gold	1 Looking for 2
Bondage Top	Grey	Bondage Bottom
Daddy	Hunter Green	Looking for a Daddy
Likes Drag	Lavender	Drag Queen
Has Tattoos	Leopard	Likes Tattooed Guys

Wants blowjob	Light Blue	Gives blowjobs
Has a dildo	Light Pink	Wants a dildo
Suck Ma Pits	Magenta	Armpit Freak
Cop	Medium Blue	Cop-Sucker
Alfresco Sex Top	Mosquito Netting	Alfresco Sex Bottom
Has 8" or More	Mustard	Wants 8" or More
Fucker	Navy Blue	Fuckee
Uniform Top	Olive Drab	Uniform Bottom
Anythang, Anytime	Orange	Not Tonight
Spits	Pale Yellow	Likes other guys spit
Piercer	Purple	Pierced

Fists	Red	Wants a fist
Shaver	Red/White Stripe	Shavee
69-er	Robin's Egg Blue	69-er
Smokes Cigars	Tan	Likes Cigar Smokin' Guys
Genital Torturer	Teal Blue	Wants Genitals Tortured
Cuddler	Teddy Bear	Cuddlee
Gives golden showers	Yellow	Likes ta git golden showers

LURLEEN'S RECOMMENDED INNERNET SITES (some'll inform ya, some'll amuse ya, but some'll just plain scare ya!)

www.aidsquilt.org	The Names Project
www.bearornot.com	All about bears! This ain't fer the young 'uns!
www.capalert.com/capreports	This bunch'a creepy Christians rate all movies according to their own idea of decency. For example, didya know that *SpongeBob Squarepants: The Movie* has 'suggestions' of sadomasochism, transvestism an' drunkenness? Dang, sounds like ma kinda movie! Check out

	what they say about your favourites
www.c-h-e.org.uk	Campaign For Homosexual Equality
www.dreamlandnews.com	The place ta read all about John Waters! There's even a picture'a yours truly on there!
www.dykesonbikes.org	Dykes on Bikes website
www.falwell.com	Jerry ain't with us no more, but his nastiness lives on
www.godhatesfags.com	These folk make Jerry Falwell seem like he was a liberal!
www.goodvibes.com	Real excitin' sex shop – check out their g-spot vibes!

www.jennifercamper.com	Real cool site for a real cool gal!
www.mccchurch.org	For all ya religious folk out there, go check these cool Christian folk out!
www.olivia.com	For gay gals who want a vacation, or any kinda info or fun.
www.queernationny.org	Mighty innerestin' reading about lgbt stuff in the USA
www.sh-womenstore.com	Beat the crowds at gay pride an' order sexy stuff online here
www.stonewall.org.uk	Stonewall organisation website
www.tht.org.uk	Terrence Higgins Trust website